PERFECTING
YOUR PLATFORM

TRANSFORMING YOUR STAGE PRESENCE INTO STAGE POWER

PERFECTING YOUR PLATFORM

TRANSFORMING YOUR STAGE PRESENCE INTO STAGE POWER

DEB SOFIELD

Firefly Printing Press ~ *Lighting your world one word at a time.*

Copyright ©2022 by Deb Sofield

Firefly Printing Press

Library of Congress Cataloging-in-Publication Data

ISBN: 978-1-64184-765-0 (eBook)
ISBN: 978-1-64184-764-3 (Paperback)

EPIGRAPH

You can speak well if your tongue can deliver
the message of your heart.

John Ford

DEDICATION

This book is dedicated to my mother, Mary,
who believed in me and always has.

TABLE OF CONTENTS

FROM STAGE PRESENCE TO STAGE POWER TO STAYING POWER

This book isn't for everyone. It isn't for beginners. It isn't for wallflowers trying to summon the courage to find their voice. It isn't for those uninterested in improving their speaking game or who aren't willing to put in the time and effort to keep polishing their platform and finessing how they do what they do.

This book is for those among us, like me, who live to speak and speak to live.

A decade ago, I wrote *Speak without Fear*; now my goal is to help speakers master the professional speaker circuit and speak boldly enough to make a living. In other words, I've written this book for the people whose audiences are waiting. They've spoken a handful of times or possibly a bunch and realize they need to polish their platform presence. Their job, career, or passion depends upon it, even demands it. They've been at it awhile, toured as speakers even, and are in the process of fine-tuning their delivery. They've done a single TEDx event and wandered the halls afterward wishing to further charm their audience and keep the momentum going.

If you're anything like me, you learn by doing. While there's a lot to be said for hanging in there and staying the course, there's also much to be said for catching your breath, pinpointing where you are and comparing it to where you want to be. So, welcome to the world of perfecting your platform and transforming your stage presence into stage power.

Make no mistake! One can either accept who and what they are or lead the charge to revise and become something better, something more polished, uncompromised, possibly even essential. The "become" is the tricky part; with this book, I want you to lift your nose from the grindstone, evaluate how far you've come, and compare it to where, farther down the road, you want to be.

For true "I-have-something-to-say" speakers, what I offer in this book are directives to tauten the learning curve in evolving from good to powerful. Look at it this way, it's nearly impossible to make an impact if all your efforts are running on all cylinders. The most intrepid will stumble along until they get it right, or don't. But if it's important to them, they keep at it. They soldier on. They stick it out. They keep on keeping on.

I've been "keeping on keeping on" for over thirty years. What I offer isn't a set of Cliff Notes. There's nothing abridged or abbreviated. This book is where what I have learned through my decades on stages around the world meets what today's speakers need to engage distracted, even non-listening audiences. Beyond excellence, a big part of being a successful speaker is having the confidence to take responsibility for your audience and making sure they're comfortable. Sure, you want to be easy to work with, you want to be invited back, but it's about having control of things like room temperature and knowing you've the right to ask that the volume of your microphone be turned up. Be a master of ceremonies, of sorts, and create the best environment for your audience.

As speakers, especially those who are content creators, the goal is to impress an audience enough to have them pay attention, because — and this is something I believe so fully and completely that it's become my mantra: One speech can change lives. What we, as speakers, put out into the world is personal; it matters. It takes confidence to present with power; it takes time, and it takes practice. No matter how short-lived or lasting your limelight, make it count.

In this book, we will first cover initial distinctions one should master before they make their way to an awaiting podium. A storyteller's boldness matters. Speakers cannot afford to be unoriginal in their messaging. We will also examine how speakers' individualized platform awareness regarding today's ever-changing social media can coalesce alongside "best practices" of speaking, how to curate one's platform, and how to gauge its impact on audiences. We will review practical aspects of speaking, such as timing and its effect on audience experience, and take a microscopic-level approach on how to craft speeches and how to continue to finesse your performance and hone your communication skills to ensure top-drawer responses for any situation. We'll examine speakers' individualized platform awareness regarding today's ever-changing social media architecture and highlight ways for speakers to fully embrace and protect their personal unique "brand." In other words, before sharing knowledge that might encourage an audience to make a change or to learn something new or buy a product, a speaker must define and celebrate who they are right now at this moment. More than any single trait, a successful speaker is one who's authentic.

We will move on from there to review why being a dynamic storyteller matters and how speakers cannot afford to be unoriginal in their messaging. We'll then examine speakers' individualized platform awareness with regard to today's ever-changing social media architecture and highlight ways for speakers to fully embrace and protect their personal unique "brand." Following chapters will dive deeper into the "best practices" of speaking, how to curate one's platform, and how to gauge its impact on audiences. We'll be considering the practical aspects of speaking, such as timing and its effect on audience experience. From there, we will move to take a microscope-level approach on how to craft speeches and how to continue to finesse your performance. Finally, readers will hone their communication skills to ensure top-drawer responses for any situation, be it on stage or in the management of their lives.

For public speakers, *Stage Power's* takeaways include the following points of fact:

✓ It is incredibly difficult to manage a speaking career.
✓ Who you are as a person is as important as your message.
✓ Cancel culture happens to creators who lack integrity.

✓ Your platform strategy must be strong enough to engage audiences and, when necessary, flexible enough to pivot.

✓ Being able to "read the room" aids a speaker in gauging their audience's experience, guiding how their audience reacts, and, ultimately, ensuring what your audience will retain.

✓ There's power in whichever stage your speaking career presently finds you; every stage is different, and every stage is a foundation for the next.

There's an old entertainment industry adage about "bit" parts which states, "There are no small parts, only small actors." I'd argue that, like Dabbs Greer, a bit actor, who once said that "Every actor, in their own little sphere, is the lead," impact isn't necessarily defined by the number of lines assigned to someone or the size of the theatre or the fellow actors with whom they perform. We all have the potential to make each moment count and the potential to steal the show. What it comes down to is having what I call stage power, and no, stage power isn't what electrifies the lights and microphone.

What I have deemed "stage power" can be likened to "star power" or the "it" or "wow" factor. Having stage power is the ability to be a powerful force on stage. Like stage presence, stage power isn't necessarily easy to describe, but it's easy to spot. The difference is that unlike stage presence, such power isn't necessarily contingent on natural charisma or charm. Stage power is possessing the power and skill to draw in an audience and command that audience's full attention. Again, more than any other trait, being a successful public speaker is at its core the ability to tap into your authentic self and share it with others.

In addition, stage power as a term is the reminder that the stage itself has power, the power of opportunity. Every single time you're on stage, it holds power, the power to encourage an inimitable moment wherein transformation is possible, and progress is possible. If I've learned anything, it's that one speech, given well, can change the speaker's life and the lives of those who have come to hear you speak. When a speaker is comfortable being themselves, on stage, something entirely special happens. That moment, that opportunity, is why learning to be a better speaker matters.

PART I

YOUR PERSONALITY IS YOUR PLATFORM

1

ROCK-BOTTOM CONFIDENCE

*The point of existing day in and day out
is to become more of who you are.*

I f there's one thing I've learned, it's that people want to be inspired. The demands of everyday life are exhausting. We all have bills to pay and mouths to feed. We worry and fret, and we get bogged down. Whether it's to renew or revise or maybe just to reinforce how they see, understand, or navigate the world, people are hungry for inspiration, encouragement, and camaraderie. People want to be moved. They want to participate, learn, and contribute. They want to be engaged. They want to be enticed and entertained. People want to know they matter, and that they too can make a difference, and they want to know more about others who are affecting change, paying it forward, and doing things in their own distinct way.

Years ago, during a book signing event after a speaking engagement, a man cracked a joke that, "I was worth the hour drive," it had taken him to travel to see me. Since then, it's been my mantra. I practice and practice and rehearse and rehearse. It's repetitive but I want to make sure what I say is worth an hour drive to see and hear, because with any given hour, we all have something else we could be doing with our time. In other words, we aren't forced to listen to one another, so when someone makes an effort to see us and hear what we have to say, it's special.

Most every religious text has a version of this phrase as a reminder that "We are fearfully and wonderfully made." I believe this. I believe this for all of us. From the ancient text of the Hebrew language, the word, "fearfully" translates *with great reverence, heart-felt interest*; "wonderfully" translates as *unique and set apart.*

Most every religious persuasion points out that we, as individuals, are unique and set apart; with this in mind, shouldn't we use what we have, our gifts, our power, our persona to better the world around us? Let me make it simple for you. The answer is yes, we should, and with this painstaking awareness hovering in the air, let me pose another question: Why would you do anything that doesn't allow you to shine as the brightest light? Besides, if there's one thing, I've learned along the way it's that no one ever loses when they light a path for others.

I can't stress enough that, ultimately, you just need to be you, the best and most confident version of you. If you want people to pay attention and not look at their phones or talk to their neighbor while you're on stage, along with being thorough and knowledgeable, you have to be different than everyone else. Whatever it is that makes you unique and unusual and not like anyone else, that's what makes people want to listen to you.

DON'T CHANGE WHO YOU ARE

In this world where viral content can take a person from anonymity to stardom in a few hours, in my experience, it takes a decade to be an "overnight" success. Yep. When it's all said and done, those who find success have spent years and years in preparation. The upside is when you do the work and you and your message finally "hit," the financial worry, emotional hardship, loneliness, and pain it took to make it happen will have been worth it. There's not much sweeter than to see your product, especially when that product is you, in the marketplace and seeing your audience better off because of it.

I hear a lot of people talking in this world, but I don't see a lot of people listening. Everyone wants to be a millionaire or land a recording contract or star in a movie, and while these dreams are great, stop and think about the few who actually make it. They didn't just start singing.

They've been practicing all their lives for three minutes of opportunity. Before they had three minutes of opportunity, they did the work, most of them anyway, so don't buy into the invention that someone was "discovered." Most likely, that someone has been working on their craft for years and now it's simply their turn. The trick, I think, is parlaying three minutes of opportunity from the potentiality of "fifteen minutes of fame" to a lifetime of something special.

We all have more than we think we do, and when we're willing students of life, our confidence comes from inside of us. Every day we read of some up-and-coming voice we'd never heard of who became a star in their own right overnight. Jamie Kern Lima, #50 on *Forbes'* 2020 America's Self-made Women list with a net worth of $460M, is one of the current "it" voices. In 2007 she and her husband penned a business plan on their honeymoon and the following year they co-founded IT Cosmetics, a problem-solving line of 300 products. They sold it in 2016 to L'Oréal and Jamie Kern Lima became the first female chief executive officer of a L'Oréal brand in the company's history.

If you know their story, it was hard-fought. She and her husband got up and slayed the dragons every single day until they, against all odds, were able to break through the noise. One suspensive instance along their nail-biting path, perhaps distressing is a better word, was when an investor went so far to say, "I don't think anyone is going to buy makeup from someone who looks like you and is your … size." She'd been a news anchor, had won a competition to appear on a *Baywatch* episode, and was crowned Miss Washington USA, but she wasn't skinny, and she wasn't a model.

QVC didn't think she should model her makeup line. Much like Sarah Blakely, when she pitched a Neiman Marcus buyer to carry her patented Spanx undergarments to replace girdles and did a "before-and-after" modeling in the bathroom, Jamie Kern Lina insisted she take off her makeup on a live broadcast so viewers could see how the makeup worked to cover up her rosacea, a skin condition she suffers with that causes reddish, blotchy skin. Her struggle with rosacea is the whole reason she'd begun dabbling in corrective beauty products, and in January 2012, she wiped concealer off her face on TV for the first time.

Her new book, *Believe IT: How to Go from Underestimated to Unstoppable*, shares her journey of how she overcame self-doubt and went from struggling waitress to billion-dollar entrepreneur. I don't want to compare apples to oranges; she self-admits a battle with insecurity and there's no doubt the beauty industry tried to bully her into towing some ridiculous beauty industry standard stereotype. I want us to focus on what initially distinguished Jamie Kern Lima and why she's successful, and that's her authenticity.

Sally Hogshead, chief executive officer of How to Fascinate and member of the National Speakers Association Hall of Fame, says it best when she tells us, "You don't have to change who you are, you have to become more of who you are." A key to being a successful headline speaker is having confidence in your authentic self. It's what separates the good from the great. Ultimately, being authentic is what inspires us. I can teach you all of what you need to master public speaking and be in front of an audience, but if you don't have confidence in who you are — your authentic, "true-to-you" self — you won't ever be great.

Put it this way: if you picked this book up because you want to be a great speaker, and yet deep down you question who you really are and what you stand for in your message, friend, you will fail. As sexist as it sounds, save the metaphor, having the sort of confidence in what you're peddling that you're willing to appear on TV without makeup (or show off your figure pre-Spanx) to make your point is indispensable.

Some folks know who they are but are overly concerned with what the rest of the world thinks. These people spend a good deal of time cowering in uncertainty or mimicking their peers in order to fit in. It doesn't always have to be that way—some people figure themselves out as they get older. You shouldn't feel chained to the person you've always been because it's never too late to find your voice and start using it. Maybe you've been quiet your whole life, but now people are noticing you. Hear me when I say: You're not average. You're amazing, and if you have something to say, now is your chance to shine. Think about some of the well-known speakers of our day, whether it's Tony Robbins, Brené Brown, Eric Thomas, or Iyanla Vanzant, they, over time, grew into themselves and are much better speakers for it.

To me, the point of existing day in and day out is to become *more of who you are*, and becoming confident—fully loving, accepting, and believing in yourself. People who are authentic and genuine and understand who they are, have the surest foundation on which to build a successful life. Oh, yes, self-awareness is a wonderful thing because it leads to self-love. A solid sense of self-confidence allows you to truly harness your power, which is essential for real success.

Self-confidence can grow in many mediums. Perhaps there was someone in your past who repeatedly reminded you that you are fearfully and wonderfully made, that there's no one else in the world like you out of 8 billion people, and that what you have to give to the world is essential. That is the belief you need to be the kind of speaker that people want to hear. You must craft a message that is so true, so curious, so encouraging, that it reaches those who others have left behind, and encourages those who are on the right path. To do that you have to believe that you can, and you must. No matter where you live, no matter who you are, no matter what you look like, you have an amazing opportunity to give others hope, encouragement, direction, and knowledge. This is how you can help others make the world a better place; you must believe in yourself and share your gift.

Whether you were born with self-confidence or it's in development, if you keep looking for the light, you will be able to reflect a light so bright that others will find their path in the darkness. And isn't that what you want to do? Isn't that what brought you to the stage? Isn't that why you've embarked on a career that scares most people to death? Yes! What an amazing opportunity you've been given. Your bedrock of self-confidence is the foundation that is not going to waver when the going gets tough.

Some speakers who lack that bedrock of self-confidence use other speakers' material. They don't trust their own abilities and doing this further erodes their belief in themselves. Self-confidence grows from the hard-won wisdom of being an original because you landed upon an idea that would help others, and because deep in your heart you care enough that you feel called to share. The people who get invited back are the people who are constant lifelong learners with an ability to encourage others to find the best in themselves, their genuine self-confidence inspires others.

Let's say we're all on a plane, and the plane is going down, and I say, "Hey, who can land this thing?" You can raise your hand and say, "I can. I'm confident," but on behalf of the passengers, we'll take a hard pass. You haven't put in the work. It takes 250 hours of flight time to be eligible for a pilot license. Self-confidence isn't a magic bullet, and as important as it is, self-confidence is only a part of the confidence pie. The other components are courage, hard work, state of mind, and always doing your best. Confidence is being certain about the truth of something. It's a feeling of self-assurance that arises from appreciating one's own abilities and having a sense of one's true north. Confidence comes from knowing you've put in the time to create a masterpiece, wherein you are the masterpiece.

FIND YOUR CONFIDENCE DIAL

They say once you've hit your first homerun, it's easier to knock a ball out of the park a second and third time. You get the hang of it. You know how it feels, so you recognize the sweet spot. When you believe in your ability, the voice in your head changes its tune. The air around a confident person is electrifying. Everyone has it in them to bring something different. Your confidence dial shouldn't contend with anyone else's.

When your passion for your message outweighs your fear of stepping up to bat, whether it comes naturally to you or not, it shows, and take my word for it, its delivery gets easier with time. It all comes down to muscle memory, and it's the same with public speaking, building your platform, creating meaningful content, and getting your point across.

The commanding voice each of us has in our brain *is* your confidence dial. Learn to pay attention to this voice and how to amplify it. Whether you're hosting a podcast, livestreaming on Instagram, speaking in front of colleagues, or leading a Zoom conference call, turn up your confidence dial, before you engage an audience. There is nothing more powerful than the use of your voice to command a room. How often have you thought about how you use it? There's no such thing as a bad saxophone. There're a lot of bad saxophone players, but the brassy, woodwind horn itself can't be blamed. There's a lot we can't control in life, but we can control our breathing. Breathing gets into the unconscious. We can calm ourselves into confidence.

We all have the ability to commandeer our confidence. I call it flexing one's spirit. It's what you do in the moment before someone takes your picture. You show the camera your dazzle. One's confidence dial is a little like stage makeup, it highlights your best look. It's how you stand up a little straighter when you shake someone's hand and look them in the eye.

This is the sort of flexing I want to see. I want you to secure an exaggerated perception of who you are at your core and then share it with your audience. You are accentuating your good qualities. You choose what you want your audience to see and hear, and that's your confidence. Flexing your spirit should happen every time you stand up to speak. This is how you engage your audience and make them receptive to what you have to say.

This skill matters more than ever, so the minute you step into the lobby or walk to your desk to turn on your camera, take time to flex your spirit. Become the most enhanced version of yourself. It's all about your presence. Powerful people take up physical space; they appear larger than life. Whether you're on a panel or serving as a keynote speaker, no one else is you. No one has your exact background, education, or family and friends. By amplifying and reinforcing your authenticity, you heighten your audience's experience.

When you enter into a situation in that state, you are really ready to rock a stage; you will have cleared the self-doubt from your mind and made space for receptivity and growth. You'll learn something new every single time you speak, whether it's learning how to navigate the stage, how to walk on, how to walk off, what you wear, what microphone suits you, how the lights should work, how the sound system should work, how your book table is set up, or mastering the camera.

All too often, I overhear other speaker coaches tell their clients to imitate so-and-so. That's a terrible idea for a lot of reasons. Number one being: You're not any of them, so why pretend to be? Nobody wants to see you imitating Barbara Corcoran or Deepak Chopra or some other speaker; they want you, so don't be someone else. Karl Lagerfeld nailed it when he said, "Personality begins where comparison ends." Your entire platform rests on your personality, and you will be successful because it's unique and wholly you.

Consider what Peggy Noonan said in her book, *Simply Speaking*: "Some communications professionals will tell you there are specific gestures to use when you make a speech, particular ways to move your hands or use your voice. I do not think this counsel is helpful. Be yourself in your presentations, because although there have already been a Vince Lombardi and a Dan Rathers and a Jesse Jacksons, [sic] there has never been you before. So, you might as well be you and have a good time. Authenticity isn't just half the battle, it's a real achievement."

Here's a truth: The key to successful speaking is being confident in your authentic self, which is what makes people want to listen to you and your message, and then take the action you suggest. If you approach an audience with the belief that you are not enough, that you need to be like someone else in order to succeed, they will sense that. They will know, on some level, that your confidence dial is not turned up. People listen to you because they like and trust *you*, your knowledge. Your life experiences are why people have come to hear you — the real you.

"LIKE YOURSELF" LIKEABILITY

If Gallup polls tell us anything, it's that when a person runs for public office, likeability is more important than a candidate's stance on key issues or their party affiliation. Historical data shows that regardless of how the public graded issues or with whom they stand party-wise, the candidate with the highest likeability factor typically wins the election. In other words, we vote for the person we like best, and it doesn't stop there. We do business with the people we like best, and generally speaking, if people like us, they will want to hear us speak.

As an elected official, I've learned a lot about likeability and how it can make or break a candidate's chances of winning an office. During my first campaign, when I was going door to door for the first time, I came to a small home with a well-maintained yard. As I was walking to the front door, a lady opened it and said, "I'm so glad to see you, Deb Sofield. We went to high school together." I'm thinking, *Do I recognize her? Is she a past friend or foe? And please tell me I was friendly to her in high school.* After a few minutes chatting, she told me I was one of the nicest people in the school, and she would be happy to be a part of my campaign, and yes, I could put a campaign sign in her yard. Likeability: It pays off when you least expect it.

So, what is likeability? My paraphrased definition is simple: Make everybody feel like a somebody. Put another way: Create space wherein people feel good about themselves. If you consistently set out to be genuine, positive, and respectful, people will like you. Now, beyond instinctual traits of genuineness, positivity, and balance, I offer a few pointers I've learned along the campaign trail.

- ✓ *A smile goes a long, long way.* As my grandmother always said, "More than diamonds or gold, a smile carries more weight than any piece of clothing." A smile alerts others you're approachable and friendly. A smile makes your best first impression. A smile also leaves your best calling card.
- ✓ *Call people by their names.* Acknowledging someone by name conveys to that person you think they're important and are worthy of your time and attention.
- ✓ *Maintain eye contact.* Faraaz Kazi, who's India's version of Nicholas Sparks wrote, "Eye contact is way more intimate than words will ever be." Eye contact is associated with credibility. It's vital and denotes attentiveness. As far as body languages go, eye contact is by far the most powerful way to make someone feel recognized and validated. It's also the easiest to accomplish.
- ✓ *Ask questions.* Nothing strikes the matchbox of inspiration like a matchstick of "tell me more." Asking questions creates meaningful relationships.
- ✓ *Know who to touch and who not to touch.* Physical touch can be important. There was a time before the Covid-19 pandemic wherein handshakes with a stranger were welcome and often

thought to cement a new relationship; it's a fact that nonsexual touching causes the human brain to release oxytocin, which stimulates other feel-good hormones, but there are those among us who aren't touchy, feely people. When that's the case, pick up on their cues.

✓ *Don't be a jerk.* Whatever you say, say it nicely.
✓ *Leave a solid first impression.* The best way to leave a solid first impression is to know your material inside and out.

Most of these pointers seem like common sense and have the power to get someone elected to public office, and yet, we can be likeable and do absolutely everything right, but for some, it won't ever be enough. Sometimes people will dislike someone for the way they walk or talk or look. I've said it before, and I'll say it again: We can't be everything to everybody. And that's okay.

It's cool if you don't like me. I'll tell you what, let me go ahead and make this clear: I like me enough for both of us. I want everyone on the planet to be able to articulate a similar sentiment. Everyone should like who they are, because no matter how many other people like you and your message — no matter how many followers you have on Instagram or Twitter or TikTok — if you don't like yourself, nothing else will matter, not ever.

So, while I always want for all of us to create spaces where we acknowledge and honor others, what I want for you above any and everything else is to have "like yourself" likeability. In other words, I want you to like yourself first and above everyone else. The world is diverse. There's room for all of us. For far too long, we've had a world, and this applies to women especially, if not specifically, where to some extent or another we've been conditioned to fold into ourselves in the hopes of being likeable in the hopes of fitting in and not rocking the boat.

My grandfather had a saying: "Don't worry about rocking the boat, because once you're in the water, all boats rock." In other words, we're all on this cosmic ship together, and your buoyancy is what allows you to set sail. Your personality is your platform, and, dear reader, I hope you use your platform to educate others and enrich the lives of everyone in your harbor — indeed, everyone at sea.

2

PLATFORM AWARENESS

The whole of you is your platform, and your
platform wholly exists to engage and interact
with your audience.

A few days after I began serving on city council, while waiting in the lobby to see my chiropractor, the TV was tuned into the "City of Greenville" channel. You know the drill, a loop of images and informational videos featured local haunts, specialties, novelties to the town, colorful images of downtown, the bridge, Main Street, and popular restaurants. Occasionally, a photo of each current council member would flash on the screen. When it happened that my photo came around, I puffed up with pride. There I was on the big screen. It was then, upon seeing myself, it struck me that Sonny and Cher's "Gypsies, Tramps & Thieves" was playing, albeit softly, in the background. Let that sink in.

> *She was born in the wagon of a travelin' show*
> *Her mama had to dance for the money they'd throw*
> *Grandpa'd do whatever he could*
> *Preach a little gospel*
> *Sell a couple bottles of Doctor Good.*

Now, to this day, it makes me laugh, but more than anything, I don't want to be perceived as a gypsy or a tramp or a thief. I mean, if my efforts are to be summed up as a soundtrack, I'd choose Bill Wither's "Lean on Me" or Randy Newman's "You've Got a Friend in Me." Choose your theme song, create your color palette. Being self-aware enough to control how an audience perceives you is the foundation of platform awareness or at least a semblance to the start of it.

What I want you to do is see, feel, and hear how you want to be perceived, and I want you to articulate this before you hit the stage. Think about how you want your audience to feel after you've left the building. When the audience member is home, having dinner with their family, what remains? Is it a feeling of evolution or even revolution? Is it one of empowerment?

Platform awareness is knowing what your audience needs to hear. It's mostly about your message, but it's also, to some extent, about how you go about delivering that message and who you are as a human being. The learning curve isn't tough when it comes to your platform, because the best way to build your platform is to build on something you know something about: You.

I have had the good fortune of working for the US State Department, and they send me around the world. I am a foreign adoption, so I fit in in certain countries a little better than others, and that's where I train. And I will say it is amazing because when folks in the Middle East tend to look at me, they see someone who looks familiar. Although I sound like an American, I look like an American, I am Lebanese by birth and many folks in the Middle East can pick me out of a crowd because of my heritage.

Your brand's value is the sum of who you are. In the speaking business, it doesn't take long for folks to put you in a box. This can be good thing. If your brand is strong enough, when people see your name, they will want to hear what you're talking about this year and next.

Think about this, you've spent years trying to be memorable to audiences, so you will be invited back. Your brand is what lingers in the minds of those who have listened to you and made a judgment as to whether they'll continue to follow you or not. When your followers, based on the power of your brand, see your name on a list of speakers, they choose to stay and listen to you.

I've been in the business long enough to know that when I look down at a list of speakers at a conference, there are those I seek out to learn from and there are others I will walk right on past. Their brand has never been developed in a way so that I know what they're going to speak about, most of them are a one-and-done-type of speaker, and like most people, I don't have time for them. Now, speakers who are lifelong learners, who continue to explore new ideas and concepts will keep me coming back year after year.

When a speaker's brand hinges on a commitment to amaze and engage, their audiences will continue to shell out money to listen and learn from them. This does not happen organically. This does not happen through advertising or even speaking. You can't "buy" attention anymore, you must earn it. For a speaker to have a long and robust career, over the years, her brand and her platform will need to grow and evolve. I cannot name a single successful speaker able to expand her platform without first defining and refining her brand. To build loyalty and create trust, a speaker must be able to clearly articulate who she is.

YOUR "BRAND" SETS EXPECTATIONS

I run with a close group of friends. A few years ago, we came together to celebrate one of our mate's last rounds of chemotherapy. As true steel magnolias, we convened at her beach house. Nearby there's a little island we love to go to called Shell Island. As the name implies, it's a favorite spot to look for shells, so we decided to take a canoe up the inlet for an afternoon picnic.

We'd been there a few hours and had enjoyed our time in the warmth of the sun when we decided we needed to get back. Our friend couldn't be out in the sun very long, but as I got the boat ready, I noticed that, although we'd caught the tide on the way out, in a matter of a few hours everything had changed. Not only had the tide turned, but an ominous black cloud was rolling in from the Atlantic, and a storm was heading our way.

If you know me well enough, there's a side of me that when I feel threatened, I become so focused and determined that even my voice changes. You might say it's part of my "brand," and it sets a clear expectation. My friends know me well enough that when they hear "that voice," they listen, and though I am the youngest and physically strongest of the group, collectively we had a determination of spirit to protect our sweet friend who could not row or even lift an oar.

We worked in tandem, rowing one side, then the other, against a powerful swell. There was no time for error, and following my direction and by working together, we beat the odds. We beat the ocean. We beat the storm. And when we landed on the dock, it was only then we realized what we had done.

If you have ever spent time in the salty marshlands along the Atlantic, you know the power of nature. She is not to be defied unless you are able to make a plan, find a leader you trust, and power through for a worthy cause. Such an experience is not unlike the pressures of being a speaker. After you leave the stage, your "worthy" cause will be remembered because it will be the legacy of leadership or actionable items you provided your audience.

Remember, if you plan to be a successful speaker with a long career on today's circuit you need to be known for something and being known for being silly hats or funny antics or feel-good stories that evaporate when your audience leaves the building and heads home with no opportunity for action in their lives you have forfeited your opportunity to be a life changer. And let me brutal: Anyone can play on the stage; only those with an authentic message will be remembered after the stage lights have been turned off.

If you don't provide your waiting audience with some sort of plan to move forward with success, I doubt they will ever trust you at the helm of their life for a direction to lead them to the safety of the shore for success. Keeping with my theme, you're just like every other shell on the beach – nothing worthy to take home and admire.

Just like piloting the boat to the shore, in truth all my friends were able, but they trusted the one who knew how to fight the waterway and push against the tide. There was no time to sit around and vote who would be the leader, the leader was already known. That's authenticity.

So, what's your brand?

Every speaker has a brand, my brand has developed as I've gotten older and matured in the business. I am known and always have been known for having high energy and being a fast-paced motivating speaker. I have been blessed with a good wit and humor. I also have a good ability to explain things in simple, concise terms where other people tend to go on and on. I've been told repeatedly I am one of the few speakers who can lift their audience to success with self-belief from the foundational truths I teach. Without a doubt I am a true advocate for those who believe they can change the world and I help them achieve their goals. Because of the work I do, I like to say I help people find their voice and teach them how to use it. These concepts are my brand, they are who I am and what I believe, and I can say without a doubt, this is my brand; it is what I'm known for, and it is the legacy I am building. Everything I have built falls under public speaking.

My platform has been built for many, many years on public speaking, presentation skills, how to deal with the media, and more recently, crisis communication and by "more recently," I mean the last ten years. Through the years I noticed I could teach everything someone needs to say from a stage or in front of a TV camera, but because the world changed, I needed to help protect my speakers in instances of crisis and that brought me to the world of crisis communication training, which is a perfect fit for how to deal with the media and public speaking skills.

My career and platform are built on the foundation of what I know and who I am. What I'm known for and what I strive for is to be relevant and actionable. What do people know about you? What do you want people to know about you? Is how you define yourself the way others define you? Are you capable? Are you flighty? What expectations do you have of yourself? What can others expect of you?

In a blog titled "define: Brand," Seth Godin offers this definition:

A brand is the set of expectations, memories, stories, and relationships that, taken together, account for a consumer's decision to choose one product or service over another.

If the consumer (whether it's a business, a buyer, a voter, or a donor) doesn't pay a premium, make a selection or spread the word, then no brand value exists for that consumer.

Zig Ziglar was one of the quintessential speakers of all time. Zig was not his given name. Originally, he was Hilary Hinton Ziglar. Zig was a stage name, and it does stick in your head. In his day he was the foremost salesmen teaching the masses how to sell. His style was tremendous. He started loud, got quiet, then returned to being loud again, and then he would end with a lilt in his voice. He is very well known for his quips and quotes. Many people in the speaking business got their start listening to the Zig Ziglar, copying his style, and reading his best-selling book, *See You at the Top*. Zig was known to be one of the foremost motivational speakers, beyond how he taught how to sell, he taught how to live a life worth living, a life of value, one that was devoted to family, God, and country. Several enduring quotes are attributed to him.

- You can get everything in life you want if you will just help enough other people get what they want.
- You don't have to be great at something to start, but you must start to be great at something.
- People often say that motivation doesn't last. Well, neither does bathing; that's why we recommend it daily.
- Remember failure is an event, not a person.
- What you get by achieving your goals is not as important as what you become by achieving your goals.
- Expect the best. Prepare for the worst. Capitalize on what comes.
- If you aim at nothing, you will hit it every time.

His philosophy was to help others reach their goals. His entire career as a motivational speaker promoted the philosophy that helping people — giving people what they were looking for, be it a product or service — would lead to success. He practiced what he preached. He extolled the virtues of integrity, hard work, and keeping a positive attitude. He had a formula: Prepare extensively every time, be funny ("Every seven to nine minutes I'll have them laughing") and frequently reinforce the broader message ("I make certain that every five minutes I'm giving them a concept, an idea, a process, a hope builder").

"Our whole philosophy's built around the concept that you can have everything in life you want if you will just help enough other people get what they want," he told Brian Lamb in an interview for the C-Span program "Booknotes" in 2002. "That works in your personal life. It works in corporate America. It works in government. It works everywhere."

He began speaking to sales groups in the 1950s but couldn't afford to do it full time until the 1970s. Though Dale Carnegie, best known for *How to Win Friends and Influence People*, was a pioneer of the self-improvement genre decades before Ziglar, an argument could be made that Ziglar was one of America's first motivational speaker successful in creating a brand.

For our purposes, you, the speaker, are the brand. There's nothing novel about this. It isn't as if the idea of a speaker being a brand is novel. Zig capitalized on this over seventy years ago. All it means is that as a speaker your brand hits a target audience, and your audience is drawn to certain aspects of your personality, from how you look to your level of success and your number of failures.

We could dissect the brands of any number of today's top speakers, but let's take Tony Robbins, who's considered by many to be the most famous speaker of all time. If we had to describe his brand it's big, it's in your face, it's warm, it's loud; he jumps around a lot, high energy, crazy things like walking on hot coals. Tony Robbins coaches some of the highest paid people in America, because he put a program into place that helps people achieve their best, while they are highly guarded secrets and they are, because you have to pay to attend his events.

He still gives to the community bits and pieces of his wisdom that helps the everyday person find a place to shine in this world. While I admire him, he's not my favorite speaker. I prefer Jim Rohn, whom we will examine more closely in a later chapter. Jim Rohn was Tony Robbins's mentor. I like Jim because I've quieted down as I've gotten older and hopefully wiser or perhaps, he's just more my speed.

I have watched a new generation of young speakers become famous, and as long as we have an Internet, they're always going to have an audience, until they walk away or are forced out by a social media mob, what I find curious is that many of them have no legacy. They pop-off Instagram-worthy comments, they have Twitter mindsets, their ADD is celebrated as success, and yet if you look closely, you don't see many followers whose lives have been changed. You see followers who are looking for a quick fix by following these influencers instead of spending years of hard-earned hard-won wisdom that builds success.

You have to have something deeper. More than 160 characters. There's no substance. It's fluff, and there won't be anything left in their wake. They didn't break new ground. Brené Brown breaks new ground. Seth Godin breaks new ground. I break new ground. You should break new ground too.

SPEAKERS BUILD PLATFORMS BY BEING PRESENT

When I was young, my dad decided I needed a part-time job and that this part-time job would be working for him at our family's recycling paper plant. Suffice to say, it wasn't a glamorous gig. It was on the bad side of town, so sketchy, in fact, that we never went there at night or on weekends unless the place was on fire or the river behind it had flooded, and as a general rule, it was smelly, and during the summer, it was unbearably hot and even smellier.

You see, the way the plant was set up, a driver would pull onto a scale with a truckful of newspaper and cardboard, and it was my responsibility to weigh it. Afterward, the driver would drive off the scale, empty the newspaper or cardboard onto a conveyer belt, and then drive back onto the scale, wherein I'd deduct the weight. Drivers were paid based on the difference of a full truck and an empty one.

All too often, a driver would take their load of newspapers and soak them with water and then put dry newspapers on top of those wet ones, so when they came on to the scale their newspaper or cardboard weighed a lot more due to being wet and then they would unload them, hoping no one was paying attention. They piled them on the conveyer belt that put them into the baling machine and then they drove back onto the scale, and of course, it weighed a lot less since the wet papers were now off the truck.

In time I got really good at watching how people unloaded the paper and how the employees would give me the high sign that these papers were soaking wet, so then we'd have to have a conversation that they could either pull the paper off the conveyer belt and put it back on their truck to dry out and come back or we can make a fair guess right then on the price. I never forgot those who spent more time cheating instead of doing the right thing.

Cheating doesn't work, or at least, it won't work for long, especially as a public speaker, because at some point, someone will unload whatever it is you're hauling. Some of us have a heavier load than others, but whatever it is you carry is yours to share.

I want you to think about your platform as a truckload of you. Tons of it, big heaping piles of DNA, your DNA, your authentic, linear self. The imperfect you, that's fearfully and wonderfully made. The no-cheating, no mimicking-someone-else you. The you that's not watered down or modified or trying to be something you're not.

Now, I want you to take a jump. This jump transcends you, as an authentic individual, and catapults you to your platform. The whole of you is your platform, and your platform wholly exists to engage and interact with your audience. No one creates a platform in a vacuum. We create and build our platforms to share ourselves with an audience.

Every single platform exists to convey something to someone. Whatever those moments of conveyance contain, there are givers and receivers, and for those moments to matter, both the giver and the receiver must be mindfully present. You and your platform aren't worth a hill of beans if you and your audience aren't present and genuinely involved in giving and receiving.

Look at it this way, have you ever been talking to someone on the phone, and you know they're not paying attention to what you're saying? You're pouring out your heart, you're explaining something, you're telling a great story, but you get a halfhearted response.

Now you know if they were really paying attention, they would be right with you, they would tell you it's going to be okay, they would question your questions so together you two could come up with an answer, or they would laugh at your amazing story. Believe it or not your audience knows if you were present with them while you were on the stage, and they can tell if your mind is a thousand miles away.

There's really nothing worse than a speaker who gives the same speech over and over with a complete disregard for who's in the audience. How does it make you feel? Like they didn't care? That's what it makes me feel like and I committed years ago that the minute I hit that stage, I'll leave my troubles at the door.

The reality is that the audience, although they like me, they don't care about my troubles, they've got plenty of their own, so don't drag your emotional baggage to a stage. I know some speakers have made a living out of unpacking their broken life in front of others so they can get a tear, a clap, or even an amen but I have to ask did it help your audience? Nine times out of ten the answer is no. Was it interesting? Absolutely. Watching a train wreck is always fun if you're not in it, but the fact is they didn't come to watch a wreck; they came to be healed, helped, or given a bit of hope.

When you're going through the motions of your amazing talk, but you're truly not present in the moment, your audience senses this, and I guarantee it will show up on your speaker evaluation, and it doesn't take too many of those remembrances to kick you off the roster for the next time.

Listen, you wouldn't want your surgeon to be thinking about his golf game as he's taking out your gallbladder. Being present in the moment, reading your audience, anticipating what could happen in the audience while you were speaking, it's not surgery but it's close. Remember one speech given well can change your life and the lives of others and that is why you must be present in the moment before you walk on the stage. Leave your troubles in the hotel room, turn off your cell phone and don't pick it back up until you walk off that stage and are either in your taxi going to the airport or back in your hotel room, because when you're done speaking, they want to speak to you. Always be present as you present.

Being present is, by far, the most meaningful way to be in the spotlight. As a speaker, this means being mindfully present with your audience. It's an act of purpose, and it means being wholly present in the moment. If you're plan is to be in the spotlight, and since you're reading this book, it sounds like it is, I want you to start thinking about what that means. Social media has changed how we exist. For public speakers, it doesn't just change how we market ourselves and how we secure paying gigs and get our content out there, it essentially changes how we live.

THE DIVINE PLATFORM

I fell in love with speaking when I was younger. It was pretty much the only thing I was really, really good at. Math wasn't my forte. Science didn't hold my interest. Sports really only works if you're outstanding, but speaking, speaking can change the world, and I can think of no better career than the one I love to do every day.

People often ask what it's like to live in the spotlight and what it's like to feel comfortable on a stage. Both are fair questions, and for me, both are amazing. Most days, at least. Being under the spotlight on stage is a powerful feeling. What's become apparent to me is that one never knows that what they've learned in life until they share it with others.

When your "stage presence" empowers your audience, encourages them to build their careers or meaningfully change their lives or, the most rewarding, get through a particularly tough time, it's magic. This isn't to say it doesn't take a lot of hard work to get there, and it isn't to say that it doesn't take a lot of hard work to stay there. Add to the equation that there's no template to ensure success. You can have a hugely powerful platform and still be an awful person. Again, it might work for some amount of time, but look at Bill Cosby, Harvey Weinstein, or Kevin Spacey. Sooner or later, if you choose to be in the spotlight, you will be scrutinized. That's fair, right?

What I want you to think about beyond whatever else you and your platform might become is that it includes two key ingredients. These include:

1. Empathy
2. Compassion

Empathy is a feeling of awareness toward other people's emotions and an attempt to understand how they feel; compassion is the emotional response and creates a desire to help.

The etymology of "compassion" is Latin, meaning "co-suffering." Compassion literally means to suffer together. Simply "feeling" for others is empathy but writhing around the ship's deck in response to another's pain, that's compassion. No matter what else you bring to the stage, make sure your platform rests in humanity.

Let me add to the human part of your speech. I came across a version of this saying a while back that sums up how we, as speakers, need to speak to our audience. This is from my crisis communications training, but it is valuable for anyone taking the stage in today's climate. The key to survival in a crisis (or on the stage to reach and change your audience) is being able to have a clear, concise, and consistent message that conveys empathy, compassion, and humanness to connect with your community.

Your life on the stage will advance ten-fold if you remember to incorporate the ideas of empathy, compassion, and humanness. Speaking to suit yourself will almost assure the shortest career you will ever have, and for what purpose? Remember, it is not about you but how you lift your audience to a lifetime of success.

PART II

"UPSTAGING" YOUR PLATFORM

3

THE UPSTAGED SPEAKER

Your audience doesn't want you to be perfect,
they want you to be present.

No one wants to be outmaneuvered, outshone, or upstaged, certainly not a speaker and certainly not by another speaker. So, while we can all be our own worst enemy, anyone whose goal it is to be a public speaker should make it a point to outdo themselves every single time they take the stage. This is something to which I've given a lot of thought.

Most speakers tend to overthink things we see from the stage. If we're not careful, we misread our audience. I remember once I had about 500 people before me. I noticed they didn't move. I saw no physical movement. They didn't shift in their seat. They didn't elbow their neighbors. They didn't so much as scratch an ear. It was strange. I became more and more animated because I'd thought maybe they'd fallen asleep.

By the time I was done and received a standing ovation, I was floored. I hadn't anticipated this. I also hadn't anticipated the people who came up afterward. They said things like, "Deb, I was captivated by your message," and "Deb, I couldn't believe you were saying the things I've been thinking but hadn't been able to put into words."

In a recent podcast, Brené Brown spoke with Grammy-winning singer-songwriter Brandi Carlile about her new memoir, *Broken Horses,* which is an intimate narrative on how music shaped her life. To me, all of Brené's and Brandi's content, be it a song or speech or book or podcast, is transformative. I could go on and on about the power of their messages, though their mediums are distinct, they're two of the most powerful storytellers of our time. At a point in their dialogue, Brené offered that, "Somewhere inside of me is a sweaty palmed Brené, holding on to a cafeteria tray with nowhere to sit." Before Brené had a chance to expound, Brandi immediately responded, "Same. I want to go back there and sit with you."

What I want to consider, for our purposes, is imagery and how imagery is an invitation. As a speaker, your job is to tell a story, and it begins with an invitation to listen to it. Whether you're presenting your budget for next year or pitching a new client, never approach a speaking engagement as if your job is merely to transmit a list of facts. If you tell someone a list of facts, they'll most likely forget the list. If you teach them, they'll have a better chance at remembering, but when you involve them, they learn.

Think of what language and imagery you present to your audience that will best invite that audience to fully listen. Image-based words offer a better chance of inspiring your audience to cooperate. The goal of using imagistic language is to help your audience create a mental picture of what you're saying. People remember what you say when you paint a picture. Imagery allows your audience to see, touch, taste, smell, and hear what's happening. There's a world of difference in saying something smells nice and saying something has the earthy smell of fresh-cut grass.

Every time a speaker takes the stage to share what's in their heart, there's an opportunity to exact transformative change, meaningful shifts in how our audience thinks or feels or reacts. Songs have this power. Theater productions have this power. A speech has this power. I have this power. You have this power too.

So, how had I mistaken attention, enthusiasm even, with apathy? How had I misread my audience? It's the whole point of what I was doing on the stage to begin with. It never hit me my audience was captivated, spellbound. While I was on the stage, since I'd seen no signs of life, I thought they weren't listening. This misunderstanding

— my misunderstanding — led me to be much more animated than I normally would have been. I believed so much in what I was saying that I doubled down, as it were, and it made a difference.

And that's the point. I pushed myself in the moment. I did what I could to upstage myself. Sure, it's clear I misread the moment and we'll talk in a later chapter about reading your audience, but for now, I want you to think about upstaging yourself each and every time you pick up the microphone.

You have a message that you have worked on, you know beyond a shadow of a doubt your audience needs to hear what you have to say, so now you have to be fully present in the moment when you're speaking. I'm expecting that you will be exhausted when you're done, why? because you gave it your all and then some. Speakers who do halfhearted speeches get halfhearted results, your audience expects more, and you should give more. I'm not saying wear yourself out for the sake of being overly energetic or Chicken Little excited. But I do believe it's important that you impart knowledge, wisdom, understanding, and you mix that with kindness, caring, and a sense of humanity. This is what will make your audience better, and, friend, that's your job. Ultimately, as a speaker, you are to leave your audience better than you found them.

What I mean by upstaging yourself and your platform, isn't limited to what and how you present yourself on stage, it's also a directive to surround yourself with positive people and to be organized, because when you've thoughtfully and meaningfully aligned yourself with positive energy, you're better able to focus on what it is you're passionate about.

Don't worry about anyone else. Realize that if you want to grow your business, you have to be better, cleverer, funnier, provide some new or updated information, a little more over the top every time you walk on that stage. If I've learned anything from being on the stage, it's that your next client is in your audience. Without fail, nearly 100 percent of the time, I've landed another client. I didn't go in there to search for another client, but when you put the effort and energy into your talk, ten out of ten times, someone will approach.

I speak to A to speak to group B and C and D and E and F. If you aren't good, you won't get those other opportunities. If you don't, you're limiting yourself. If you don't hit that stage a little bigger, a little better than you originally planned, you'll limit your opportunities for other jobs.

I get pumped up with the Bee Gees. I'm staying alive until I get to that stage; you want to do something to kick your heart rate up a notch. If your speech is about grief, this might not help, but I crank up rock and roll. A hymn ain't gonna cut it. You feed off the energy of the audience. That's also why the person who introduces you matters.

No audience member has or will ever look at their watch and say, "Gosh, I hope this speaker is awful. I hope for the next hour I'm bored. I hope she leaves me uninspired and without hope." I'm being serious. No one hopes you flop or you're awful. Why? Because they have to listen to you.

Before you arrived at the venue, someone had the foresight and the confidence in you to invite you. They wouldn't invite you if they didn't believe that you have something important to offer. Your audience wants you to succeed and do well, so accept this as something that's working for you. This is one of the greatest gifts you can receive as a speaker, so bask in your audience's preemptive goodwill.

Audiences want to be engaged. They want to be enticed and entertained. They want to participate, learn, and contribute. People want to know they matter, that they too can make a difference—and they want to know more about others who are affecting change, paying it forward, and doing things in their own distinct way.

Mastering your content is key. Once you do, the speech becomes a conversation more than a presentation. Don't overly prepare. If it sounds like a rehearsed speech people zone out. People respect people in their industry who know their stuff; people also prefer speakers who aren't reading from a teleprompter or a set of slides or directly from their prepared notes. Think about what it means to be animated, dynamic, enthusiastic, and vibrant. Whether you're speaking to twenty-nine people or five hundred, the energy demand is the same (except with an audience of hundreds, you must project your voice and energy louder). Nothing else. Master the stage. Get your act together.

When you're speaking to say, thirty people, a small audience where you can actually see your audiences' faces, it goes without fail that out of the thirty, twenty-nine think you're amazing, and one wonders why you're even there, they make silly faces, act bored, huff and puff, doodle on their paper. They don't pay attention. If you're not careful, you will ignore the twenty-nine and beeline focus on the one. I'm here to tell you stop. Ignore them or they will do great damage to your psyche. You don't have to be liked by everybody. I know this is hard and when you are standing to speak you are so distracted by the one person who is making funny faces, acting bored, and rolling their eyes, instead of the others who are so grateful you're there. Please hear me, focus on the good; don't let the one nutjob ruin it for the others.

In the past, like many so many speakers, I have overly focused on a single waste-of-time audience member (who came because they were as forced to attend for their organization). I have had to train myself not to look at or engage them. Instead of a stare down, I dismiss them in my mind. Frankly, I would invite them to leave if I could, since I don't want their "gutter" attitude to affect others.

On any given day, at any given hour, any audience member could be doing anything else, and yet, they have chosen to come and hear you or me speak. They have chosen to sit in an audience and listen, and depending how long you speak, most will stay with you until the very end, and if you're good, you'll be rewarded with a standing ovation. If you're not so good, they'll clap politely, and if you're terrible, they'll walk out, never come back, and they'll tell others not to come.

Stop and understand this dynamic: Today's audiences have unrealistic expectations. Hourly, they're fed made-up, perfectly curated drivel spewed from the taxidermized lips of television personalities who consistently and flawlessly look amazing. So, when you and I show up live, in person, we're held to their standard. Unrealistic expectations are on you that you must meet. I will never look like the folks on TV — most speakers don't — and that's okay. Your audience doesn't want you to be perfect, they want you to be present. Life isn't a dress rehearsal, and mine isn't a canned message. My value is in my message. It's all I have, and it's all I need. The only thing that matters is that my message lifts my audience to a place they haven't ever been before.

MAKE AN ASSESSMENT

Between my junior and senior year in college I had an internship with a large political group in Washington, DC. At the end of the summer, they asked if I would stay on and finish my education in DC.

Coming from South Carolina, it was a whole new experience to ride a subway to work, eat at food trucks, go to the Capitol maze of buildings for meetings. My major in college was public speaking and you had to dress appropriately for every presentation, so at a young age I had beautiful clothes, and the look of a young professional and because of that I was chosen repeatedly to attend evening events to serve as a hostess, partly because they knew I would show up and leave sober. That reputation landed me a lot of nice comments and a job opportunity.

Excitedly, I called my parent to the share this awesome news. I'd been offered a job with a great organization, and I was going to make my mark in the world. The conversation went something like this:

Me: "They offered me a job."
Dad: "You need to finish school here at home."
Me: "No, you don't understand. They offered me a job."
Dad, "No, Deb, you don't understand. You need to finish school here at home."

I hemmed and hawed a few more minutes, and then, after a long silence, he repeated that I needed to be home by Thursday, because I had class on Monday. To say the least, I was unhappy. Who was he to tell me what to do? I had a job offer. How many people get a job offer before they graduate college — and in my dream city of Washington, DC, where I was going to change the world? I wanted to stay. I figured I would work my way up in this organization and, one day, be a star. I was sure of it.

What my father had done, and I'd failed to do, was assess how my future would play out. My parents knew if I did not graduate that next year, it would take me years to get back on track. You see it over and over in Washington, DC, where smart, dedicated interns get low level jobs in hopes of an opportunity for advancement, but due to not having a degree in whatever the job was asking for, they are stuck at the bottom of the pile or going to school at night while working days. While my story is not unique it still recalls that in every situation, it's important to look beyond the current situation to see what could happen down the road.

Dutifully, I showed up home on Thursday to begin my classes on Monday. Years would pass before I was able to admit being able to make an assessment is critical to one's success. In my case, it was finishing a job I had started. In the life of a speaker, it is being wise enough to look down the road and see where the landscape is being created and as a speaker will you be part of the growth or be left behind.

Let's say I were to hand you a microphone. Let's say there are a thousand people waiting for you to speak. Let's say you've made your way to the stage, the spotlight is on you, your notes are in front of you on a lectern, and you've been introduced. Now what? What's your opening line? What's your message? How will you capture your audience in such a way that they put their mobile phone in their pocket, look up, and listen? Are you ready? Make an assessment.

If you've been on the speaking circuit for any amount of time, it becomes apparent how to read your audience. Most audiences, when we start are polite but about fifteen to twenty minutes into your presentation, you'll notice they start to shift in their seats, so you must shift in your speaking meaning at this point you need to have a story, a quote, or saying something that brings them back around to you and your presentation. Your assessment of how to redirect or refocus the audience to you is what will keep your audience engaged until the very end.

If for some reason you fail to make a correct assessment you might miss connecting with your audience, so consistently read and watch what they're doing. Are they talking to each other? Are they looking down? Are they on their phone? If they are doing everything but listening to you, then you've got to do something to make them stop and look back up to you on the stage. Otherwise, you're just talking to yourself.

The more you speak you will notice and understand what to see, fix, or repair. Watching actions and reactions, noticing if your audience is closing their eyes or reading the handout. The rustling of the audience distracts what they hear and feel.

Over the years, it has become obvious that most audiences cannot sit still for more than an hour without a break. I am known to give a break every hour on the hour, even if it is what I call, "the Southern twirl," where I ask my audience to stand up and turn around a few times. Why? Because movement helps refocus the human brain, and it is my job to make an assessment and keep my audience focused on my message.

THE CUSTOMER SERVICE EXPERIENCE

Think of your audience as your customers. Sure, they might not have been the ones to hire you, but whoever hired you did so on their behalf. It's not a big leap to take and by adopting an audience-centric approach, you will be able to keep your audience at the center of every decision you make.

As you would do in any transaction, you're going to make sure you get the best bang for your buck. Believe it or not your audience feels the same way; while they might not have hired you directly, they have chosen to sit within your presence, to glean the information you're sharing, and the hopefully leave the presentation and use that information to grow in their career. In the truest sense of the word, they are your customers, they're buying what you're selling so you must have a product worth taking home.

At the risk of sounding like a broken record, adopt an audience-centric approach; keep your audience at the center of every decision you make. I know this seems like a given, but the longer you're in the business, if you're not careful, the easier it is to fall back into a rut of telling the same stories and repeating the same quotes and sayings. I think it's wise for speakers to know a little bit about their audience, whether you Google the organization and its leadership or you happen to know somebody in the company or check in with whoever hired you to tell you who will be in your audience. It is a whole lot easier to keep your audience at the center of your talk when you know your audience, the basics at least. Remember, it's not up to them to be engaging; it's up to you.

Ask for feedback. When asking for feedback make sure it's from a trusted friend. Now that seems like a given, but I know many speakers who get their feelings hurt because a friend thinks they need to "put them in their place" or be "real with them" even if it hurts their feelings. Remember your friend is not a speaker. They are a listener, so they only know half the equation, you only take feedback that is positive and is easily workable into your next presentation. You understand how this business works; they do not, and while their words may have some truth, you must decide for yourself if what they share is important enough to make a change. The fact is most organizations will have a score sheet that the audience will fill out after you're done speaking, you really need to make sure you are scoring high, not only for the organization but also to prove they chose well with you as a speaker, because you've kept up with the times that your message is relevant, it matters, and it needs to be heard.

It's tempting to "check on your competition" but if you do the work, there is no competition. Now, undoubtedly, there will be other people who speak on similar topics as yours, but remember out of 8 billion people, there's only one you. That's why your message matters. That's why you must craft your stories. That's why you must do the little bit extra to make the audience remember you. Remember, it's your job to be memorable; no one's going to hand that to you.

The competition on speaking circuits is intense, so while it's human nature to compare yourself to other speakers, in truth such comparisons rarely lend itself to a strictly apples-to-apples evaluations. There's always a little something different about the person who speaks because that difference is what got them to the stage. The fact is you should not care about your competition because nobody is like you, and that is your ticket to fame and fortune.

I saw a quote a while back. I'm not sure who to attribute it to, but it went something like this, "When they ask what you do? Answer: Whatever it takes." I'll add to that this means mentally, emotionally, and physically. The other quote I really like is this: Hustle until your haters ask if you're hiring. While I know some reading this book don't like to think about "competition" or having to "hustle" because for the most part, we want everyone to succeed. While I applaud that sentiment, let me remind you that you are in a competitive business. Only so many speakers will make the stage, so the only question I have is: Have you done what is needed to be one of them?

If your career is waning because the young Turks are taking your business, you need to stop and figure out what went sideways that allowed them to take your place on the stage. Was it their perspective of taking a new look at an old problem, or their ability to rock an audience with their flash and show, was it their new book on your old topic? When I realized my first book, *Speak without Fear* was ten years old, it prompted me to revisit some of my work and create a new opportunity to keep current in the marketplace. And let me remind you that just because you are a member of National Speakers Association, or some other group, does not guarantee you a place on any stage today. Most new speaker have never considered joining NSA or other groups because they are too busy powering through the stages that will have them and podcasts that showcase their new ideas.

And if you're not on the stage, you need to ask yourself, "Why not?" I would venture a guess you haven't done what it takes to be memorable. You're good, but you've lost your edge, so keep working. If your material isn't relevant anymore or fresh, that's on you, don't blame your audience, or the committee, for choosing someone else.

Let me add in another truth about this business. Let's say you are rock star amazing and you're still not making the stage of the conferences of your dreams. Just know that other speakers will be chosen because they "friended' the person in the organization who hires speakers, it happens all the time, and while it is frustrating what you need to do is to figure out what it takes to make that organizations stage or ask to be a break-out speaker and then be so good that the audience chooses you and talks about you so much so that the staff has to go with the audience choice next time. While being lumped in with others as break-out speakers might not be to your liking it could be your best bet to create enough buzz to capture the attention of those who are in charge, so you'll have a chance at the big stage the next time. Don't dismiss the small starts if it gets you to the big stage.

When I was starting out a well-known political group came to my state. Since I wasn't known by them, they wouldn't give me a chance at their big stage. My friends who were on the board for bringing this group to our state negotiated for me to be a break-out speaker. Realizing that I needed to create some noise, I stood in the hall before my session and chatted up the conference attendees and invited them to my "amazing talk." I went so far as to ask them to please come and hear me. My friends on the conference board also encouraged attendees to come and hear me. Lo and behold my break-out small room was filled to the brim with extra chairs having to be brought in and some attendees were standing in the hall. When the national folks noticed my overflow crowd, they sat in and heard me. Fortunately, I was on fire, and, after that one break-out speech, I become one of the national organization's regular big-stage speakers and worked for them for many years.

In that case, I met and exceeded everyone's expectations. Just know that meeting customer's expectations isn't always easy. There will come a time when you've done everything right but for some reason it all goes wrong, and you will not meet the expectations of yourself or your audience; don't fear, you can get it right the next time. As a speaker we are constantly learning, you're going to have to change up your talk, add in new stories and statistics, it is your responsibility to do whatever it takes to keep your talk relevant and timely for your audience because I have found that is the best way to meet and exceed expectations.

4

REVIEW, REVIVE OR REMAKE YOUR PRESENTATION TO BE TIMELESS

*The goal of any presentation is to make
the listeners think, respond, and act.*

Be it baking or travel or comedy or storytelling or politics, when or where we're born or when or how we die, timing and preparation are everything. It's how we decide to run for public office, deliver punchlines, find true love, break one another's hearts, and yet the timing and preparation of and for any single event or series of events really only does so much. There's a world of difference between timing and how we choose to spend our time. There's also a world of difference between preparing for something and the windfalls — or downfalls — that fall in our lap. When it counts the most, time preparing always gives fate a run for its money.

For about a quarter of a century, I've been confident that how we utilize our time is far and away more important than "timing" or anything parallel to coincidence or chance. To me, it isn't necessarily about being at the right place at the right time; what matters most is that a person makes time to prepare for what one hopes to achieve. To me, timing is to time what confidence is to success and preparation is to mastery. Sure, timing has its charm and typically makes a good byline, but time is what you make of it. Time is, for most of us, something we can, at least when we honor it, use wisely.

Everything we set out to accomplish comes down to carving out the time it takes to make it happen. A pro ball player doesn't head out to the ballfield for the first pitch of the season until after spring training. A university professor doesn't show up to class before curating a syllabus and studying the material. Online influencers, and these are some folks who've really mastered timing, promote content, take time to review and revise before they post it.

A few of us might chalk our success up to being at the right place at the right time, but I'd argue that timing is a honed skill as much as it is luck. If "timing" is an eighty-year-old widow jumping into the online dating scene and landing herself a beau, than "time" is her acknowledging that finding a second love of her life would require her to put forth the effort. Another way to look at is that while "timing" does a good deal to shape our relationships, actual "time" is an active ingredient that prioritizes, shape-shifts, and demands our attention in attaining our wants and desires.

Whether you're trying to get to the next level in your profession or a new parent figuring out a new path to a second career or you're twenty-two and out to set the world on fire, when it comes to creating content, draw upon your experience. Choose information that's significant and appropriate for the situation. Make it a habit to know what you're trying to say and state it clearly.

I am a topical speaker. I have four main areas of training that I teach. These include public speaking, presentation skills, how to deal with the media, and crisis communication. I primarily teach public speaking skills to the professionals *or those who would like to be* but under my public speaking training I have a section on platform presence, I have a section on personal presence, and a section on understanding your audience.

I also teach how to deal with the media. There is a large percentage of dealing with the media in your ability to speak well, how to handle yourself in front of a camera or a microphone, knowing what to do, what to say and how to say it. The same thing with crisis communication; it's more than the words you use, it's the way you use them, how you set up your command center, what words you choose with the media and the public to show you're in charge and that you care. For me, as a national speaker and executive speech coach, everything falls under my core message, which is public speaking skills for the professional. And if you want a long career, I encourage you to consider this type of format for your long-term success.

I am not all things to all people, so instead of writing a new speech each week, I am always in search of a new audience, but my audiences come back over and over and over again, because they know they will always learn something new that I will share with them.

While I always coach people to have a single concept in mind, it is equally important you understand the concept of finding a unifying theme. When speaking events fail, often, it's that the speaker did not understand that, in addition to imparting information, a speech must move people. When you're preparing your speech, think about how it will affect your audience and, hopefully, move them to action — the action they must take, so they're successful and their company or organization is successful. The goal of any presentation is to make the listeners think, respond, and act.

Some speakers have so many different messages, they're not really known for one big idea or one big theme or message. I'm not saying you need to lock into one thing or solely commit to a single topic, but your message must easily reflect some of the other themes of your topic. Not everybody does, but if you're plan is to have a long career, at any point in your career, you can branch out and create new material while still being connected to the old.

Brené Brown does this beautifully. After developing a theory on shame resilience, she elaborated on the power of connection, studied what she called "Wholehearted Living," "The Gifts of Imperfection," and vulnerability. Whether or not this was by design or one thing leading to the next, from her 2010 TED Talk on vulnerability, she's gone on to share relatable, reliable data and anecdotes through speaking engagements and five number-one New York Times bestsellers.

When I think about messaging, I ask this question: What is your message that ten or 10,000 people need to hear? What are your main points? What are you going to leave your audience with that they will remember and hopefully use in their life for their success? What is so life changing, informative, instructive, or educational about your message that they absolutely need to hear. Why does your message matter?

If you didn't give this message, who else would do a good job? Have you perfected it so much that it is a part of your persona? Does it reflect who you are in your real life? Is it such a good fit that we can't imagine life without one or the other? What do you have to say that matters? That, my friend, is your message and when it comes to preparing new content, draw from your established wheelhouse; your message is your mission.

Start with a Single Concept: The Agenda of "So What?"

Since you're reading this book, it is assumed that you're a professional speaker or would like to be, and while I am going to spend a few pages on some basics, please note I do this because your audience has changed. They are not listening, or they are listening half-heartedly. Our world is full, and your listeners time is limited so allow me to review some basic reminders on how to capture and keep their attention for your speaking success.

Beyond how you look, how you sound, and what you say, to the audience, it comes down to answering the question most audiences are asking and that's "So what?" Consciously or unconsciously, your listeners are asking "So what?" Most everything you say and your job as a speaker is to answer this question throughout your talk. How does this affect us? Why do I care? Why should I care? Does anyone else care?

When you speak, it's up to you to be interesting enough that your audience doesn't retreat into their own world of what's for dinner, who has carpool next week, and when their mother-in-law's birthday is. You know the type of presentation I am talking about. The one where the guy stands up and drones for hours about nuclear sub energy in third world countries and fails to make it relatable. Remember your audience is always asking "So what?" to everything they hear.

Having a single concept in mind means finding a theme that will help you organize your speech logically. Your audience wants you to be amazing, they are looking for information from you to change their lives for the better. You have a responsibility to do the work and for some of you that means a refresh of your standard talk. Going forward, develop one or two good new quotes, stories, and analogies, especially audience-appropriate personal ones. By now something interesting has happened on your speaker's journey, so tell me the new stories. Insert them early in your speech and maintain the central message and theme from the opening.

As you start to think through how to choose a topic for a speech, remember the basic standard questions; these never change, so keep them in mind:

1. To whom are you speaking?
2. What's your subject matter?
3. How long will you be speaking?
4. When are you speaking?
5. Where is the speech being presented?

For many of you, the topic will be given to you by your boss or the organization that's inviting you to speak. For this example, let's assume you've been asked to inform an audience about something, or you've been asked to persuade or encourage people or entertain an audience for a corporate event. Let's assume you get to speak on any topic you choose, let me give you a couple examples that can help you when choosing your topic.

As you know, the easiest way to pick a topic is to choose something you have personal experience with; it could be a hobby, it could be your travels, it could be what you do day-to-day at the office that someone wants you to explain but, ultimately, settle on something you would like to tell others about.

After you've chosen a topic, create a scattergram. Take a piece of paper and write down everything about that topic on your piece of paper. Nothing is too silly to write down. What I'm trying to do is put all my ideas in one place and then the most interesting thing will happen. Once you see all your ideas written on paper, your mind will naturally begin to put things in order. Remember, we're taking the time to add or update new information in our talk. I can't stress enough that you need to be aware of what is happening around you with regards to your topic, nothing will kill your presentation than you rehashing old information. Make time to do a new scattergram.

Again, write down everything you think about your topic. You may have questions. These you will answer. Maybe you've seen things about your topic in the news lately. Maybe a quote relates to your topic, or a famous person has the same hobby. Write down anything that pertains to your topic; everything is worthy to be written on your scattergram. I'd rather you write more ideas down and not use them, than not write enough. The more you write, the easier it will be for your brain to put things in order.

You could also go online and see the latest the Internet has to offer about your topic. If I were going to speak on Southern antiques, and I know a lot about them since I'm a former auctioneer. *(I gave it up when I got tired of saying, "Gentlemen, make me an offer.")* What I should say is that I *knew* a lot about Southern antiques. I don't know what's happening in the market today with buying and selling or the current pricing, so I would do well to go online and read up on what the current market is and what is selling and what part of the country is selling the most and what's the pricing points for pieces that I may have and is there a particular wood that the buyer is looking to buy at auction or is new furniture being made by Southern artisans. Because my topic is so big, by putting it on paper, I have a lot of ideas to choose from, but I also limit it by what I believe would be interesting for my listening audience. Remember, my goal is to answer my audience's "So what?" Remember, to appeal to our listeners, we must always answer "So what?"

There are a lot of options for you to find material to add into your talk. As a speaker I have a lot of "speaker files" I keep or links to topics I would like to write a speech about later. I keep articles that have been published in magazines or journals that can help me add more information to my topics.

Sometimes I'll hear a phrase and I think to myself that would be a great title of a speech, and I'll write it down put it in my file and years later some other word or words will come in to play and that will be my new title. I heard the phrase Misfits Mavericks, and I knew it was good, but it just wasn't enough, and then I saw a title about a year later that said Renegades and Rascals and I thought, That's it! What a great title! Now one of my after-dinner talks is called "Misfits, Mavericks, Renegades, and Rascals: Four Traits of Leadership." It's a wonderful talk about people in life who went against the grain, and we are better off for today.

As a speaker I must have several different talks, and this is one of my most requested. And again, I had half of the phrase in my head. I just had to wait to hear the second half a few years later to put it all together. If a word or phrase captures, you need to write it down put it in a file. You never know if one day it'll be a title for your next great speech.

I am an elected water commissioner, so I'm always online looking for new ways to clean, protect, and find new sources of water and how people around the world deal with water issues. Whether it's building a new well or I saw something really cool online the other day where they were absorbing water from the air, purifying it, and then people could take the water from a turn on switch at the bottom of the machine. I'm fascinated with turning salt water into clean drinking water; it is hard to do, but it has my interest. So, if I'm looking for a topic I look everywhere, and you should too, especially current events. The last thing you want is to be talking about last year's big invention when this year's invention is bigger and better.

After you've chosen a topic, begin to think about you might want to organize your speech. As you do this you need to ask the three universal questions all speakers need to ask as they craft their speech, so you can you put yourself in your audience's mindset to understand your talk.

1. What is it you want your audience to remember when you're done speaking?
2. What does your audience already know about the issue or topic?
3. What is it you want your audience to do?

What action do you want your audience to take when you're done explaining or teaching or talking, persuading, informing or entertaining? It is very important you think about these questions as you craft your speech.

Think about your title. When was the last time you updated your talk's title, so your title appeals to today's audience? So many times, the title of the talk is excellent, and the speech is boring. That's not a good thing. Your title should spark interest. I heard a speaker once say to think of your speech title like a movie title, short and to the point, or at least to a point of interest that makes someone want to buy a ticket to see the show.

If you can, keep your title short, so it fits on the program and any social media the organization might use to advertise you. And write down three or four fresh title options and then think about which one really speaks to your topic. I am assuming you have updated your talk from last year so your title might need to be updated to reflect your new idea or concept.

As a speaker your job is to tell a story. Whether you are presenting your budget for next year or pitching to a new client, don't approach your talk as if your job is merely to transmit a list of facts. Remember that you've chosen a topic, any story you give must have a clear point of view. It has a beginning and an end, interesting characters, a plot, good dialogue, humor, and illustration. Remember your speech is not read by the audience; they have come to listen, to watch, to feel, to become a part of that presentation. Your audience isn't reading your notes; they have come to listen and absorb your power to change their lives. That's why it's important to understand that many times your job is to tell a story that has emotion, has feeling, it can be inspiring, or a talk on gratitude or a real-life experience.

I'm sure you've heard the story of Warren Buffett the Oracle of Omaha and how he became so unbelievably wealthy after he was able to overcome his fear of public speaking. I like to tell the story because it's such a dichotomy. We see him on all the talk shows, and he's well spoken, like a grandfather, *if your grandfather was a billionaire*. I like to tell the story that Gillian Zoe Segal, author of *Getting There: A Book of Mentors* recalls.

Up until the age of twenty, Warren Buffett, had a fear of public speaking. "Just the thought of it made me physically ill," the billionaire shares in his "Getting There" essay. "I would literally throw up."

Warren Buffett said that he purposely selected courses in college where he didn't have to stand up in front of the class and arranged his life so that he would never find himself in front of a crowd. If he somehow found himself in that situation, he admits that he could 'hardly even say' his own name.

During Buffett's time at Columbia Business School, he saw an ad in the paper for a Dale Carnegie public speaking course for college students. "I figured it would serve me well," he recalls. "I went to Midtown, signed up and gave them a check. But after I left, I swiftly stopped payment. I just couldn't do it. I was that terrified."

After he graduated, Buffett returned to Omaha and got a job as a salesman of securities. But the problem still lingered: "I knew that I had to be able to speak in front of people," he writes. "So again, I saw the ad in the paper and went down to sign up; but this time, I handed the instructor $100 in cash. I knew if I gave him the cash I'd show up." And he did show up.

"There were about thirty other people in the class, and we all had trouble saying our own names. We met once a week for a dozen or so weeks. They would give us different types of speeches to practice and taught us psychological tricks to overcome our fears," explains Buffett. "There was that communal feeling that we were all in the same boat and really helped one another get through the class."

When the course was over, Buffett went to the University of Omaha and announced that he wanted to start teaching. He knew that if he didn't speak in front of people quickly, he would lapse right back to where he started.

"I just kept doing it, and now you can't stop me from talking," he jokes.

Warren Buffett credits much of his success to the class, and his office shows more than enough proof. "I don't have my diploma from the University of Nebraska hanging on my office wall, and I don't have my diploma from Columbia up there either — but I do have my Dale Carnegie graduation certificate proudly displayed" he says.

"That $100 course gave me the most important degree I have. It's certainly had the biggest impact in terms of my subsequent success," he says.

The lesson here is that it doesn't matter what career path you take — whatever you end up doing in life, the basic skill of public speaking is crucial to your success. "In graduate school, you learn all this complicated stuff, but what's really essential is being able to get others to follow your ideas," Warren Buffett reminds us.

Like all public speaking teachers, I love that story and how public speaking skills will open doors of opportunity that other soft skills won't.

I've already mentioned the idea of a scattergram. This makes all the difference in the world, especially when you're having a hard time thinking of all the different things you would like to say. Or due to the world changing new questions may have come up about your topic so here is a chance to refresh your information to be relevant to the issues of the day. I believe a scattergram gives you freedom to update, change, or grow your tired, worn-out topic or speech. Remember, you don't have to put it in proper order right away. It is a deceptively simple process that yield great results.

Then, when you are ready, create a tentative outline. Do not write this in paragraph form; we are simply looking for the key points to update and redevelop your speech. It is here you have some options. You can arrange your materials anyway you want that makes sense to you and your listeners. Maybe you will use chronological order using historical data from the founding of the company to today. A generational direction is another way. Your great, great, great grandfather who came over on the Mayflower to your great, great grandfather to your father and now you. The great thing is you have options.

I have found it easiest to state each point as a single idea and then branch out from there to make three points. Three is a magic number. We think in threes. Your audience thinks in threes. Educated people speak in threes. Think about it. Red light, yellow light, green light, go. In science, we have protons, neutrons, and electrons. In church, we have Father, Son, and Holy Ghost. And my favorite cereal, snap, crackle, pop. Use it to your advantage, and in that vein, try not to have more than three main points in your speech, as that is typically all your listening audience can handle.

Use the magic of three to your advantage. A bonus reason I like to think and write in threes is that it can help grow your talk to fill in the places where you might be thin on content. The rule of three is, for the most part, universal in every county I train in. While I am sure you have a structure you currently use, go back and review and see if you have mastered the magic number to help settle your talk in the ears of your listeners.

Being clear as a speaker ensures our messages settle in the minds of our audience, so it can be repeated and remembered. To accomplish this, we're going to limit the number of main points. Remember, the mission is in no more than three. You also need to be very clear in your transitions and make sure your language is clear and direct. I've spoken about the value of words; words have power, so choose words that are appropriate for your topic and your audience. I always want you to use words that are alive and colorful; choose evocative words that allow your audience to see and feel.

Let me ask you a question. When was the last time you learned and used a new word in your presentation? Seriously. Think about your favorite talk and then think about the last time you gave it. What did you add in that was new, interesting, unusual, current, different, funny, smart, sad, and/or engrossing?

Please tell me you did your homework and updated your talk. If you haven't updated your signature talk in the last three months, you are dying on the stage. Trust me. Someone else will take your topic and paint it with a fresh coat of current information and claim it as their own.

Let me touch on a few more issues I am seeing from the stage. In today's environment, you need to be able to show impartiality in your talk.

I know this seems a little odd, especially when you're trying to move somebody to your point of view, but today's cancel culture audience wants to know you can see both sides of an issue. While they might not like what you say, they'll expect you to have thought through the opposing side's position, so think about being a little bit impartial.

It is in your best interest to be able to explain both sides of your issue. A good speaker should be able to defend their beliefs about the topics in which they choose to speak. The problem for so many in your audience is that, if they don't know you, they feel like they need to get another opinion. By showing you are impartial and familiar with both sides of an issue, you are afforded your best chance to sway them or educate them on an issue or simply reinforce what they believe to be true.

I can tell you as an elected official, if I don't really know you and you come to me with an issue you want me to deal with, I will take what you have at face value. Although it seems right and may, indeed, be right, since I don't know you well and I don't know your reputation, I feel it's my responsibility to at least hear the other side of the issue. So, think about it if you sit with me and you give me your side of the argument and then you say, "Let me tell you what the other side is saying and here's why we disagree," now, I can weigh both sides because you have been fair, and you gave me options. That's important when you're trying to persuade someone to your point of view.

My final third point should be obvious, my friend, you have got to be interesting. In fact, you must be more interesting than you were last time you spoke. That means you've got to put in the work. Maybe it's a story, a quote, a new idea, or a thought. Maybe you've got something to show me, a visual aid — whatever you have, it is your responsibility to satisfy my curiosity or spark my interest or to teach me something I don't know. Being interesting is a requirement. Otherwise, you'll lose your audience and then word will get out that you're not an interesting speaker. That'll hurt you in the end, so be interesting. Whatever it takes, be interesting.

Therefore, I implore you to be a lifelong learner, and it is easy when you love your topic. And hear me, if you have fallen out of love with your topic, find a new one. That is only fair to your listening audience. Finding new and updated information is a joy because you know that you will now be imparting useful, current, present-day information to educate and inform and make your audiences' lives better, and that is your job, speaker.

Let me touch on another issue I am seeing most every time I am speaking at a conference. I am not sure why this is happening, except to say that travel is harder now than ever before. Family dynamics seem to be more volatile; budgets are tighter; audiences are more restless, demanding, and confrontational. The group that hired you is having a time dealing with the conference center, missed flights, poor service, sick attendees, and to top it off, the speaker who was to present is stuck in Atlanta with no flight in sight, so in a panic the hiring team reaches out to all the onsite speakers and asks if any of us can speak on another topic.

Nine times out of ten when an opportunity like this happens, none of my colleagues are prepared to step in and save the day. Here's a distinction. I am always prepared to do another presentation, even when I know I was not chosen for a second speech due to pricing, time, or some other reason. Dear speaker, consider the opportunity you have now lost because you only offer "one and done." You've been "thinking" about preparing another presentation, but you're not ready to rock the stage, you haven't put the time into your new message or updated an older speech because, deep in your heart, you never believed a phenomenal opportunity like this would come because, let's admit it, it is a once in a lifetime chance to take the stage a second time, but it might be the one (second) chance that changes your life and career.

Your lack of belief in the spontaneous opportunity to take the stage when others are not prepared has lulled you into becoming dull or worse than that - you are unprepared. So, when the time comes and you are not ready to take the stage to fill in for someone who at the last minute, couldn't come or who got sick, you wrecked your opportunity to shine because you've allowed your message to grow dull, unforgettable, uninteresting, and frankly not worthy of your listener's time. Never forget that one speech given well can change your life and the lives of others and for that you need to be ready, you never know when opportunity knocks, I just hope you're ready to open the door, answer the call, and welcome it in.

Let's get back to organizing your speech. As you're working on updated content and thinking about what you need to support the central idea. As you know, supporting the central idea is what we would consider the meat of your message. You can use stories, quotes, testimonials, visual aids, using statistics, or a specific instance that brought you to this point in your life or career. This is where you get to have your freedom to put down on paper things you've always wanted to say.

I am constantly astounded when I go to dinner with other speakers who have great stories of being on the road or working with clients or retelling some stage issue, and yet, I never heard those "laugh out loud" stories from the stage during their presentation. When I ask why, they look at me like I have a second head. Their response is usually something like, "Well, that happened to me, and it isn't something I thought others would think is funny." To which I will most likely reply, "You've got to be kidding. We're all doubled over in laughter from your trials and tribulations. Why wouldn't your audience enjoy it?

I know many of us as speakers tend to have serious topics, but please know that today's audience carries a heavy load so if in your presentation, you can take a rabbit trail or two to show the human side of you. Consider doing so. As they say, laughter is good for the soul — yours and your audiences.

If your speech happens to be long, it's a good idea to occasionally go back to the main idea throughout so your audience can follow you in a logical manner. This gives them mileposts along the way. Remember while they are listening to you, they are thinking about other things so leave some breadcrumbs, so they can follow you. Sometimes in your talk it's good to repeat some of the original phrases so someone who is outlining your talk for their notes is able to follow along. Now, you don't do it where it's overly redundant, but sometimes it's good to go back and say, "Remember we spoke about this and this and this (crime, education, and taxes), and now here is where this comes in under education." It keeps the organization logical and easy for the audience to follow.

I'm not sure how you start your speech, but I know most speakers like to give a personal story of the worst or best advice you ever got from your friend, boss, your brother, your neighbor, something personal to add a little color to their story. Let me remind you that your audience is more visual than ever before due to social media, so whenever you start with your stories describe the person who told you this advice and by color, I mean give them a name, describe what they look like, maybe describe their car or the clothes they wear or how they smell. By adding color, you bring this character to life.

Many times, I use a famous quote to open or a startling fact or figure to wake my audience up. Other times, I refer to a historical event, depending on the age of my audience, or I pose a question to my audience. Although sometimes this is overused, always do what is best for your topic and audience. Everybody loves life stories that deal with loss, failure, or success by taking the path less traveled. Think though your options and choose the one or two or three that fit with topic and what you want to impart.

You can also incorporate the age-old format of previews or a summary into your speech, so your half-way listening audience can follow. Here's an example. "Thank you for inviting me to talk about the three main issues my campaign is based on: First, … Second, … Third, …" or you could also say something like, "I appreciate the opportunity to talk today about the three main issues in my campaign." Remember, these kinds of verbal cues help your audience put together the pieces of your speech without having to think too hard, so they can spend more time paying attention to your content.

As a keynote speaker I rarely start my talk with a "thank you for having me" line because it is so overused. There is nothing more annoying than saying "good morning" when you are the third morning speaker of the day. You have thrown away an opportunity to capture your audience when you use the old worn-out speech beginnings of yesterday. Many times, I will start as I am walking to the front (I'll have a lavalier mic so I can be heard), and I will say something like, "Last Thursday at 4:59 pm my phone rang and the voice on the other end of the call said, Deb …" and then I stop (by now I am at the front behind the lectern or at the front of the stage). Now that captures an audience. I can either use a funny line or jump into the crisis my client has so I can explain how we solved it. And then after a few minutes of speaking and knowing I now have my audience's attention then I say something like, "Before I go on, let me stop and say thank you for having me. It's my pleasure to be with you." To win in today's non-listening audience environment you must capture then right from the beginning, and you do that when you craft a rock star opening line to capture their attention.

I was not great in English class, but as a speaker, if there is one thing that really turns me off, is when somebody is not clear on what they're talking about. You'll hear a speaker referred to their big idea as: it, they, this, them, those, instead of saying what it is i.e., the education system or the political process, the Bubble company; use names if you can without causing harm. If you don't use a name, your listening audience will be wondering what you are referring to and then you have lost them. Let me say it again, and I know you are tired of reading this line, but your audience is not paying attention, so you must craft clever words to awaken their mind throughout your presentation to keep them with you until you walk off the stage.

What I'm asking is that you limit pronoun use and be specific by using nouns. When people speak in generalities such as "those people" and "that organization," your audience has a hard time following who you are talking about so always be clear, and if you can, use names.

Never Ask Permission

Most of us are polite, and we like people to support us. I think all of us want to work with people who inspire us and believe in us, but we can't wait for someone else to give us permission to speak the way we want to speak or demand we speak in a certain way. Those days are past. By this point in your career, you need to have developed your own voice, not your mentors, teachers, or trainers. Your authentic voice is the one your audience wants to hear.

Everything we have to give our audience comes from within, and you, the speaker, has to decide. Whatever it is — the content, your style, your humor, your brand, your handouts, all of it — what your audience experiences, is up to you.

There's a great woman named Carol Van Den Hende. She's a marketing executive with Mars, but she's also a writer. Her debut novel, *Goodbye, Orchid*, has won over a dozen literary and design awards, which nods to her decades-long career in marketing. Years ago, when she was on the grueling path to find a literary agent, she went to what the publishing industry calls a "pitch" conference. Now, from what I understand, typically a dozen or so New York literary agents sit on a panel and a hundred or so hopeful authors are given an opportunity to "pitch" them their book projects. It's sort of like speed dating. As one might expect, these aspiring writers tend to toe the line and blend in as much as possible. Not Carol. She wears the brightest pinks she can find and brings hot pink M&Ms with her face and name printed on them. Carol doesn't ask permission to bring chocolates. She gave herself the greenlight to be exactly who she is and who she is, is a woman who stands up for herself and stands out.

So, stop hesitating. They came to hear you, to listen and learn from you, don't hide your true self; your audience will see through that, and it will harm your long-term career. Be your big, bold, self-assured, energetic self and leave them wanting more.

So, while we know nothing pulls an audience in like a personal story or an issue that you or your office has dealt with, let me state the obvious, make sure you have an outcome that is relevant to the audience. Just like your opening captured their attention, your closing must do the same thing.

As you develop your talk or are updating or writing a new one, which means preparing your content, don't forget to maintain your core points in an organized manner and remember to answer the "So what?"

Let me lay out in a very generalized format what I call a speech planning. I want to grow this idea, so you know the bits and pieces you should be considering.

1. Wake them up and pique their interest by providing a startling fact or figure or statement or you can share a brief story or example about your life that directly relates to your talk. You can start with a question, quotation, or familiar saying do something that will capture their interest.

2. State the topic. Let your audience have some idea of what the purpose of this talk is about. Are you informing? Are you educating? Are you simply entertaining? Remember every talk

has a job to do; this is where you tell your audience what your job is currently by stating the topic. Being clear and concise are the keys to a successful speech. You want your audience to know where you are going with your talk so they can follow along or you will lose them.

3. Don't forget that in the early part of your talk you've got to make your talk relatable to your audience. Remember they have come to hear you speak about a topic that concerns them. Think through the expectations, interest, and the nature of the audience.

Whether it is a common experience such as graduation and going into the world of work, or something they fear such as growing old, or not having good health, or situations that everyone goes through such as caring for elderly parents, or young children, building a business or finding the right job.

You can state your main points. Remember the rule of three. Emphasize each point with thoughtful, clear, consideration and logic. Use transitions to connect your ideas together. It helps the listener follow your thought pattern. I will always encourage you to use stories, personal experiences, or humor to reinforce your points.

As you're building your speech with these main points, I want you to include things that you've always wanted to say, you might need a photo for people to grasp the idea. Displaying a photo on the screen behind you is a great way to make your audience think and follow along with you; you might even use a video clip or maybe a bit of a song. At this point everything you say or are showing is okay to keep in front of you as a visual as you continue to craft your message. You cannot use the same old photos you used in the past; there are many online sources for you to use to upgrade your visuals and finding new current quotes, facts, figures, or current sayings or even slang (that you hear online or by others). Everything is okay because you're still in the working stage so don't limit yourself when it comes to your main points; remember they need to tell the message that only you can tell.

You will also want to include your supporting arguments here and you might want to add a new story, perhaps an outline. This is the base of your foundation of knowledge. It's much easier to delete than to come up with new information or new ideas, so put it all down. Let your mind flow and put your thoughts on the scattergram paper so we're able to organize them when we come to the time to write your speech.

Conclusion of your talk. As powerfully as you began your presentation your audience wants something to walk away with, and it's your job as a speaker when you conclude what should be the last words your audience remembers? And remember you must memorize your last words or phrase because you were looking at the audience as you give your final words.

Really try to keep to three main points and tell them and retell them as you are speaking. It is as simple as your opening, middle, your close

And don't forget the age-old truths:

- A confused mind always says no
- Last words linger
- Don't forget the magic of threes

And I'll add to the old speaker adage: If you can't tell it, you can't sell it.

PREREQUISITES

Platform awareness begins with personal perspective. Everyone starts somewhere. Perhaps your local Rotary or Sertoma club, they don't pay, but they buy you lunch, and you get to practice and if you are good enough, somebody in that audience who heard you speak might very well ask you to speak somewhere else. Speaking on a national circuit usually starts within your hometown or within an organization that you are a part of. For many years I spoke at conferences for city council members and municipal elected officials, why? because I was elected, and I understood what they were going through, I just happen to have the skill to put it into words make it interesting and give them some tools to work with their constituents, with the media, and to learn to work with each other. After a while my reputation grew, and other cities asked me to speak and then I got on the circuit for speaking at municipal organizations. While they don't pay much, I began to build my brand, and my reputation grew, my social media following grew, and today I'm on a top 100 list of speakers at municipal conferences where I now I sell my books, I sell my online class. I am now able to be hired as a private coach all because I started with what I knew and I was very good at it; in this case I had to be elected in order to be the truth teller of what those sitting in that audience knew felt heard understood every single day

And that happens when the person who hired me gives me a good overview of who was in my audience, why they've come to hear me speak, what are their expectations of this presentation. I often ask who speaks before me and after me, who introduces me, how long do I have to speak, what type of microphone will I have, do they have my handouts in their packet or do I need to hand them out at the event, will somebody handle my PowerPoint, who handles my computer equipment, is there anything else I should know? Yes, that is platform awareness from a personal perspective, and I highly encourage you to make it a habit to ask as many questions as possible to make your event a success.

Let's talk dollars and cents. I know you want to be paid the big bucks, but nobody is going to pay you if you are not a known, respected leader within your field. Because you are a speaker, since you're reading this book and this book is not for beginners, you know it is really tough to ask for that first check for your speaking engagement.

When I started on the speaking circuit in my hometown at a few events, and by the way that's how most of us get started, in our hometown, with a hometown audience, that will forgive a few missteps as we learn to master our trade. I spoke for free for a little over a year, but then I quickly got a reputation for being a really great speaker with amazing content and energy and I had actionable items for my audience. So now I had value because my audience said so, not because I said so. Big difference.

Seriously, don't think someone's going to pay you because you think you're so amazing, let me just be honest with you here my friend, they're going to pay you for content. Content they have not heard before or that is presented in an exciting new way.

Let me tell you a story that unfortunately happens all the time to speakers. For many years I had a radio show on Saturday from 1:00 to 2:00 and I had a huge listening audience in four states.

Inevitably somebody would email me and say, "I want to do what you do, I want to be speaker, how do go about it?" I tried to be polite but after a few years of "I want to do what you do," I got tired of explaining and created a three-question list.

1. If I were to give you a stage and audience today, what would you talk about?
   a. The standard reply was "I don't know."
2. Do you have a speech ready?
   a. "No, I'm not a good speech writer."
2. Is there a topic that you really like and know a lot about?
   a. "I can talk about anything."

I will never forget this one whiny guy who emailed me and said he wanted to be a men's Bible speaker, could I help him? He went to church regularly, it seemed the pastor made it easy since his sermons always had three points and a poem, he figured he could do it.

I went through my three questions with him and got the standard answers

1. I don't know what I would talk about.
2. No, I'm not a good speech writer and I'm not really good at English
3. I can talk about anything.

So, I said, what if I set up a local church and you speak to the Saturday men's group when you are ready let me know. I think it's been eight years now.

Everybody wants to speak; nobody wants to do the work. Nobody has any idea who they would really speak to if they could. Trust me. Not everybody wants to hear you. I have a friend who's really good using Google, and her response always is "I can talk about anything to anyone," but she does the sloppy work of finding three little points from Google articles, written by others and adds a couple stories that she recreates every time, they are never true, she says a couple good lines with a couple good quotes maybe tell a tearjerker story in hopes to get paid and walk off the stage. She is never invited back, but she doesn't care, she's so desperate for a paycheck she will sell her soul. Hear me when I say that years later, she's not considered a good speaker, nobody will hire her anymore, because there's no message, there is nothing memorable about her content. In fact, the content is so thin her audience can see right through it. Remember people will only pay you for actionable interesting content.

Find a topic that you know a lot about and that you love, not a topic you like or that you just pulled from Google, but one you love. Find a topic that when people talk about speakers for that topic your name is mentioned. When people talk about women in politics, women as candidates running for office my name is on a top 25 list of speakers nationwide. Why? Because I train at The Campaign School at Yale and at the Women in Public Policy program at Harvard University and am a guest on podcasts, radio, and TV shows because I know my material, I know politics and my audience knows it

You will soon learn that many speakers want to be paid for very little work, hear me that doesn't happen in this business and here's why. Too many people are trying to get into the "speaking business" because on the outside it looks fun, and you get to travel and meet cool people. The problem is most of those wishful speakers have nothing to say that anyone would pay them for. And as you know or are finding out, this is a very tough business and if you only have one main line of speaking topics and have not branched out to add in other lines of interest under the umbrella for which you are known, your days on the circuit will be short. Very short.

Let me tell you the other side of this business. I have an acquaintance who likes to say that he trains in leadership. He has had a few jobs with that title, but to meet him in person he has zero gravitas; nothing about him stands out. For being a speaker on leadership, he shows nothing in his personhood, his manners, or his ability to lead. I can't tell you how many times he tries for speaking jobs but is overlooked for jobs because he doesn't come across with any "leadership skills" although he claims that is his forte.

I feel for him. I know him. He is a good man, but he has little to no leadership skills in his personal life or from the stage. And because of that, he is not being hired. In fact, many of the jobs he has reached for have come back with the most ridiculous reasons for him not making the cut because no one wants to hurt his feelings or be unkind. Unfortunately, what he needs to hear from those he wants to work with is that he isn't a good fit because he doesn't come across as the one who can train others in leadership since he so obviously lacks leadership skills himself. Please hear me, if you are not rock-star amazing at what you want to speak about or if you don't at least look and act the part, someone somewhere will fill the gap because you did not bring to the table the goods to win the job.

When you actually have a topic and you're really good and are deeply knowledgeable and you have something to say that will help your audience, just know that nowadays you're up against the "free speakers" out there, those who are in hopes of getting a gift card or their hope is that maybe someone in the audience might to try to hire them for any of the twenty-four things they think they do well.

If you do not have a record of accomplishment in the field that you want to speak in, it is really hard to get paid in this business. If you are a naturally comfortable speaker on the stage, just because you can speak if you have not developed a following due to your knowledge, insight, and wisdom you won't get paid the money you hope to garner.

Now the second thing you run into is how much do you get paid? I know when I started out $500 was my starting point, and I hated it, but small groups didn't have a lot of money and they had never heard me speak. I didn't have a great following because I was beginning but over time, I was able to go from $500 to $1,000 to $2,500 to $5000 to $7500 to $10,000 to $15,000, and beyond. But trust me, I spent a lot of years at that $2,500 to $5,000 to $7,500 range before I was able to kick it up; it doesn't happen overnight. It might take a couple of years.

Where you are on the circuit depends on who you are and who knows you and whether you're good enough to be paid. I have a friend who often would just get paid $500. I told her she had to do better. She had to practice saying out loud she was worth $5,000 for her talk. The first time you say your new price, you kind of choke on your words because you're really getting paid for what you love to do, but you must practice out loud like it's just common conversation that your standard speaking fee is a premium.

I do not use a speaker's bureau. Some people do. If you are famous or well known or wrote a bestselling book, a speaker's bureau will pick you up. Now, they take a big portion of your check, but you don't have to worry about a thing. You just show up, speak, walk off the stage, and get paid. Most bureaus won't take beginning speakers because you haven't built an audience that would command a big paycheck, unless you're the last guy off the plane that landed in the Hudson River and had a life changing experience. In that case, the powers that be probably found him.

Because of the work I do, I don't really need a speaker's bureau to take a large percent of my speaker fees because I speak to a very specific demographic, and I coach one on one with corporate executives. I learned early on that I am not all things to all people, and I am not for every audience. You may be different; you may have an inspiration story that brings in large audiences who want to be uplifted or encouraged. That is great that you have chosen that path – the point is simply this, you get paid for what you know and the more you know the more you can command in your speakers' check.

You are going to learn that best way to be paid at the top tier is to have a book on your amazing topic. I will discuss this more at the end of the book. I remember sitting in a conference and the keynote speaker was terrible. I leaned over to a friend and asked, "How did he get to be the keynote?" She looked at me and said, "He has a book." Now the book was slightly better than his speaking, but the fact is at that point in my life I didn't have a book and watching and listening to that awful speaker lit my fire to get a book done.

I can pretty much guarantee at some point you'll be sitting in an audience, and somebody will be speaking, and you will think to yourself, how do they get to the front of the room, they're terrible and it's at that moment you'll decide. You'll either start a podcast, you'll do more social media, you might write a book, you'll start blogging and you'll soon suddenly realize that you've got to do more to be seen by those who are looking for a speaker on your topic. Because this is a very full industry, with a lot of average people, if you're good and I assume you are you'll stand out because your work will show the work that makes you an expert.

A number of years ago I happened to be looking on LinkedIn and I saw one of my friends had changed his title from social media guru to speech coach. Now I knew this guy, he was not good at social media, and I knew he was not a speech coach but since he couldn't make money at social media, he thought he could switch to speech coaching, and since he considered himself a good speaker and had spoken at a few local social media events he thought he could flip a switch and pocket some easy cash.

I will admit I was rather bold and brash when I called him and asked him when he became a "speech coach" to which he hemmed and hawed and said that he had helped another friend of ours and the friend told him that he had done a good job, so he didn't think it was harmful to put on his LinkedIn profile that he was a "speech coach".

I reminded him that if he really was a speech coach, he would have clients, not just one who was a cheap friend, I also reminded him that if he had a real client and he messed that client's speech up he would never have another client. I encouraged him to go back to being a social media guy because he was never going to make it in the speech coaching business not when I was hustling for clients, and I have a reputation of being an amazing coach. Just because he needed another source of income and wanted to undercut me financially because in his words "people can't afford you," I was not about to let somebody who would hurt up and coming speakers because he needed a little side hustle.

I know you want to make money in this business, I don't doubt it and you should make money but remember most speakers love their topics so much that they would speak for free and sometimes you do, don't be so caught up in the money game that you miss big opportunities to change lives. I know you must make a living, I fully get it, but I also know if you're really good, they will find you, and if you're average, you might make some money, but you will not make a difference in anyone's life. Don't be average. Be rock-star amazing and get paid for it.

RESEARCH THE ORGANIZATION

When I'm speaking to a corporation out of town I'll go on their website. I'll see the charities they support, what they do as a company, I also check to see what's the latest news about them. I'll Google their name and type "news" in the subject line and that will bring up all the latest articles about that corporation. I might mention their latest and greatest news in my speech, or I might not, but I always try to be prepared, knowledgeable, and informed about who they are and what they do.

When you're looking for new information to build into your speech, there's a lot of places online you can go. You can look at fun sites such as history.com, this day in history or quora.com and search for your topic information data, anything that refer to what you're talking about.

Something a lot of speakers forget to do is to ask the meeting planner to provide goals or objectives for the event. Never walk in unprepared. And to that point you need to research the organization who has invited you to speak, knowing who they are and complimenting them will be a feather in your cap. I am constantly amazed when speakers show up without knowing whom they are speaking too, either because your schedule is so full or you're just downright lazy, and we've all seen it happen when the speaker calls the organization by the wrong name. Guess what? You will not be invited back, and it will kill you in the business because the people will talk and talk and talk about how sloppy you were.

Several years ago, there was a congressman who was speaking at a Veterans Day event. I noticed his staff were uncomfortable and were trying to get his attention. I noticed that something wasn't quite right, as he was speaking to the group he was going on about their service in the Vietnam war come to find out they were Korean war veterans – yeah, that didn't go over well he didn't seem to catch on that his staff was trying to get his eye – he was an arrogant chap so in the end nobody wanted him ever speak again – and he wasn't a congressman for very long – friend figure out who you're speaking to, that is your job and it only takes a couple clicks online to figure out who the organization is and what they stand for.

Let me say this as a speaker, a couple times, I've had to send my regrets to groups who asked me to speak but because I didn't like who they were and what they stood for, so I had to decline the invitation. Do your homework. You don't have to speak to any organizations that goes against your morals and values, remember it is always your call. Learn to do what is best for you and where you are, just know, some groups don't deserve your presence.

Let me share another situation that has happened to my speaker friends and me more than once. Instances like what follows happen more these days. I will receive an email asking me to either coach or speak to a group that I would not normally engage with due to our differences and beliefs. As with any group you might not want to work with, be very careful how you decline an invitation. You do not want to be accused of being a racist or having some type of phobia that someone will label you with since you declined to speak or train with their group. If you do not handle this well, you have real problem on your hands. Most groups are upfront and honest, and if you cannot accommodate their need for a speaker, they understand. Those are the good ones. Be aware that there are others who might target you since you will not bend to their opinion. As you well know, the world has changed, and as a speaker, you need to seriously think through who you will share your gifts with. My point is simply this: be aware and kind when dealing with the public you don't know or do not have a connection with.

My next point is obvious, but it still needs to be stated make your script fit the situation. I was speaking at a small town in South Carolina and my speech was about throw the bums out and as it turned out the bums drove their wives to the dinner. It was a terrible situation I got myself into and got out of and I've never been back to speak. No doubt it was my fault and while I needed to make my script fit the situation it was an uncomfortable situation for me, and I am sure my audience. Just a note, I have never had that happen a second time in my thirty years of speaking. I learned my lesson.

You need to have an understanding of the audience's needs today and how you need to address them with your topic, so you leave a lasting impression with great information.

Okay, so now you're a famous speaker, and everybody loves you but remember this rule: There is nothing is worse than a speaker who gives the same talk to different audiences. This shows a total disregard for their intelligence, and it shows how sloppy the speaker is, and I see and hear it all the time. Don't be that speaker. Your audience knows better and so should you.

For years on the speaking circuit there was a guy who was extremely overweight. He made it part of the schtick. He told funny jokes, talked about being a heavy and living "large," then one day, for his health, he decided to lose weight and did very well. The strange thing was he kept telling all the same fat jokes from the stage because that's all he seemed to know. He himself had changed, but he never changed his talk because that's what used to get him laughs. Now, what's interesting is, most audiences didn't want to hear him anymore; his jokes didn't make any sense, and he not the jolly old guy he was. He hasn't created anything new in years, and it shows. He has little value for his audience who is looking for a bit of wisdom from his lifetime of learning. Listen, there is nothing is worse than a speaker who gives the same talk even when things have changed.

I've mentioned this before, but I'll say it again. I have speeches in my files that I do not give anymore, why? Because the world is changed and those topics aren't relevant to today's audience, even if the information is still good and may be used in another way, I am very careful that I don't do the unpardonable sin of giving the same talk when things have changed. Come on speaker you're better than that, do your work.

Things you might not initially think to ask but should:

1. Did you write that in your contract and are they are or are not allowed to use your recorded talk this one time or until time eternity?
2. Even if no compensation is available, there's value in a contract. Many times, you will do an engagement without being paid just

because you like the group, or they are friends – let me remind you that you should always get a signed speaker's contract even when you speak for free. It just sets you up as a professional and it keeps everything in order and in open about what you do, how you do it and the value you are giving them.

3. This next piece of advice everybody argues with me about, but you know it's a fine line when you're the speaker and you've been invited to the reception the night before. The group you are speaking for will most likely all know each other because they're in usually the same industry, they are old friends and they get together at these conferences and usually go for a couple drinks the first, second and third night they are there. Most groups will invite you because you seem friendly and nice and you're the speaker but be careful. My advice is to thank them but do not go to the party and if you do feel like you should at least step out for a little bit make sure you keep your bedtime you need to be in your hotel room locked and ready to go no later than 9:30 PM because reputations are ruined in minutes.

CONTROL YOUR INTRO

Nothing blows me away more than when I hear a speaker who hasn't updated their introduction and then expects the person introducing them to have done the work. My friend, if you plan to be successful, that's not how this works.

You know the things you've done that make you amazing, and you are the only one who can put into words what your audience needs to know about you. The best part is, it's great when other people tell the audience how rock-star cool you really are. It's hard for you to do that without sounding egotistical or full of yourself, but by all means let others do it for you. You'll sound awesome and they will be successful since they know what to say about you, so now you're both set up for success.

Look at it this way. If you give someone your resume, they will pick and choose a few things that are important to them and maybe not you. Our resumes have our official records of work, but they don't actually show the real stuff, the real you the creative, outrageous, interesting, person that you are and that's why it's important you write your introduction. Write it out and send your introduction in advance to the person who'll be introducing you.

And if you speak in your hometown, like I do sometimes, with people who know you, they stand up and say things like, "Well, our speaker today is Deb Sofield. Everybody knows Deb. Here's Deb." And that's all they say. What they don't say is what I've done, especially what I've done recently, like teach at Harvard and Yale, and work at campaign schools across the country, and I work for the US government by way of NGOs (non-government organizations) in other countries. They don't say any of that because I'm "just Deb," a friend of theirs. Unwittingly, they fail to set me up for success.

I have three introductions I carry with me. The first is my serious, everything-I've-ever-done-in-the-world "resume" introduction. My second has humor. I made it funny so the audience would laugh along with me and get a glimpse that I'll be a fun and engaging speaker. The third is an amalgamation of the two. It's a bit of the work I have done in my business and professional life with a couple fun lines about me, but it's not nearly as long as the first full "resume" intro that has everything in it.

You have a choice here. You can choose which introduction to give the person introducing you or you can give them a chance to choose which one is best for that audience. Either way you'll control the opening narrative that helps sets the stage. By the way, in all my years, whenever I hand my introduction to the person who is going to introduce me, I have never had someone say, "No, let me make it up." No, they were glad to have something to work with, so they too sounded professional as they took the stage to introduce me.

Never leave it up to chance. People who are asked to introduce you don't mean to be sloppy. They just don't know any better, and frankly, they rarely say the things you want them to say. And nine out of ten times, they forgot to bring the introduction you emailed them. So always carry your introductions with you, so you will be set up for success every single time.

Just a couple other points, make sure your introduction is on your stationery and is at least twenty-point type, so it is easily read by the person introducing you.

Occasionally, you'll be asked to speak, but you will not have been introduced, meaning somebody says, "Deb, step up here and say a few words." Mark my words, it'll happen at some point in your life, because you are a "famous" speaker, and when it does you might have to self-introduce. Trust me. This happens a lot to speakers, so now, today start to think through a couple things you think your audience needs to know about you.

Some things you can say: "It's always good to be back home," "Last time I spoke here...," "I'll always remember when ...," "As many of you might remember, my mother headed up the PTA ...," "As I was driving into town, I was struck by how different things are from when I grew up here," "It is so good to see Miss Jones, my tenth-grade English teacher. I know she is as surprised as many of you are that I actually turned out well." Your main purpose is to remind them in a very nice way of your importance.

A Sample Introduction (Deb thinks this is too long and a bit boring)

Deb Sofield is a dynamic keynote speaker and executive speech coach with over thirty years of experience in training women and men in public speaking, presentation skills, crisis communications, media skills, and message development in the US and abroad. She is the CEO of Executive Speech Coaching, a private speech coaching company with decades of experience helping clients become effective, powerful communicators. As a former advertising agency owner, Sofield blends visual and verbal messaging that wins at every level. For many years, she was host of "Encouragement for Your Life" on the Salem Radio Network. She has been seen on "The Today Show," CNN and many other network news shows and has been published in leading journals including Palmetto Physician, Upstate Business Journal, Greenville Business Magazine, *and* Council of State Governments Magazine *and many others. She is the author of the book,* Speak without Fear: Rock Star Presentation Skills to get

People to Hear What You Say, and her new series, Encouragement for Your Life – *Tough Love Memos to Help You Fight Your Battles and Change the World. She is a visiting professor, teaching public speaking at Harvard University's Kennedy School of Government, and on the faculty of the Campaign School at Yale University, where she is past president of the board. She has worked at Loyola University School of Mass Communications, the University of South Carolina's School of Mass Communications, and Clemson University. For years she worked with the International Republican Institute and served on the board for the Women's Democracy Network of Washington, DC and served as a mentor and trainer for the Center for Liberty in the Middle East. She was honored by Leadership South Carolina with Legacy of Leadership Award; additionally, the Southeastern Institute for Women in Politics awarded her the Leading Women Award. She was also awarded the Order of the Palmetto, the State of South Carolina's highest honor. Ms. Sofield is a Liberty Fellow, affiliated with the Aspen Institute Global Leadership Network, a worldwide community of successful, high-integrity entrepreneurial leaders. Ms. Sofield is the Commissioner of Public Works for the Greenville Water System and the first woman to hold this position since its inception in 1918 and a two-term member of Greenville City Council.*

Her topic today is How to Deal with the Media in the Age of Twitter. Now, help me give a Texas size welcome to our guest speaker the Honorable Deb Sofield.

A More Reasonable Sample Introduction

I am happy to introduce our guest speaker today, the Honorable Deb Sofield. Deb is a keynote speaker, author of the book, Speak without Fear: Rock Star Presentation Skills to get People to Hear What You Say, and her new series, Encouragement for Your Life – Tough Love Memos to Help You Fight Your Battles and Change the World Radio, Talk Show Host in the Salem Network, Podcaster and President of her own Executive Speech Coaching Co., which trains women and men for success in speaking, crisis communications, presentation skills, media and message development in the U.S. and abroad. Recognized for her work for improving the lives of others, Sofield was awarded the Order of the Palmetto, the State of South Carolina's highest honor. Deb Sofield is a visiting professor, teaching public speaking at Harvard University, John F. Kennedy School of Government, and on the faculty of The Campaign School at Yale University, she served on the board for the Women's Democracy Network of Washington, DC. Sofield taught Communications and Media Training for Civil Society around the world, and she served as a mentor and trainer for The Center for Liberty in the Middle East. Sofield represents the City of Greenville as a Commissioner of Public Works for the Greenville Water System and is the first woman to hold this position since its inception in 1918. Sofield was formerly a two-term member of Greenville City Council. Her topic today is How to Deal with the Media in the Age of Twitter. Now, help me give a Texas-size welcome to our guest speaker the Honorable Deb Sofield.

As we are beginning to craft your speech let me continue to talk about a few things that the audience will notice about you... remember once you're on stage it's all about you. That's why having an introduction that set you up for success is so important. The next most important thing is your audiences' first look at you once you approach the lectern to begin to speak.

5

MAKE IT A PRODUCTION

Ask far as idiomatic expressions go, when we say someone "makes a production" of something, it isn't good. You know the type. It puts people off when a person makes something more complicated or difficult than it needs to be, so the trick is to make your delivery seem effortless. It's a show. Step into it. A good speaker has already walked into it beforehand, but it's good content that gets your audience to act.

NOTHING STICKS LIKE A STORY

The older I get, the more I realize I don't have all the answers, not yet at least. What I have are stories, lots and lots of stories. They're not long. In fact, most of the time, when I retell them, it doesn't take me more than a minute, but then, I've crafted them. I've cut them down. Ultimately, what I do is make them stick.

A story that "sticks" is one that makes an audience feel something, and what they might feel runs the gamut. This could be indignation or disdain, even rage, and it could be joy or encouragement. Again, stories that stick, be they informative or entertaining or both, should make people feel something. Maya Angelou was a woman who gave her audiences a lot to think about. One thing guides me with every speech I've ever given. and offered that "I've learned people will forget what you said, people will forget what you did, but people will never forget how you made them feel," and help us process things.

When it comes to stories, I use them for humor, for direction, for inspiration, and most of all for learning. Nothing is as easily taught as a story. Be they cautionary or archetypal, whether they're linear or share a viewpoint, it's the easiest way to get one's point across. When it comes down to it, beyond the oxygen and carbon, blood, and bone — in other words, the atoms that give our human bodies shape — we're stories, you, me, everyone, and all of us.

People love to hear somethings that's relatable and personable; it makes it believable. What's valuable to you is a story, or at least, it has a story. A story is nothing more than an account of something. For our purposes, it's an experience you've had that you want to share for a reason. It might be your why. It might be your when. It might be your "This is how I survived."

In my family, as the youngest of five — the only girl and adopted — I was bound to have a few "remember whens." We all have them. We all have stories in us, and it's glorious when you sit down and think about it. Look, no one else sees the world the way you see it. No one has had your particular and specific vantage, and so no one can tell your stories quite like you.

The problem with retelling most of our stories is we haven't crafted them to make them usable in public presentations, and while there aren't any hard, fast rules, there are some hard, fast guidelines I'd like us to cover.

For instance, when it comes to crafting a story, Rule #1 is, ideally, it should be your story. A couple of years ago, a lady started her speech by telling who she was, who her people were, where she came from. She said, "I am the daughter of …, who is the daughter of …, and she did this whole litany of supposed family members. It was fascinating until I heard it at another conference from another speaker and another and another. The truth is I don't know who started it, I don't know who copied who, I do know by the fourth time I heard it, I was sick of it because I didn't believe any of it and neither will your audience.

About every ten years the idea of "storytelling from the stage" comes around and all the speakers start crafting stories that are highly embellished and mostly not true and really don't have a purpose except to make them the speaker sound amazing and then "storytelling" goes out of style and then ten years later it comes back again. Clearly, I don't have a problem with storytelling — storytelling has been my bread and butter my entire career. I do have a problem if your story is not true, if it's not about you, if it's somebody else's story (and you don't give attribution), or if it is a story, you just made up because it was convenient.

Let me give you my list when it comes to crafting a story:

1. It needs to be a story about you or someone you're close to or even maybe some story that's been handed down, but you must have a connection to it.
2. If possible, make sure it's true.
3. It must fit with your presentation. Just because it's funny doesn't mean it makes sense in your presentation.
4. Make sure it's not long. Nobody wants to hear a four-minute story.
5. Audiences appreciate startling facts and figures.
6. Don't tell other people's stories.
7. If you do tell other people stories, at least give them credit.

I like to tell my audience the story about Governor Ronald Reagan when he was the Governor of California. Seems he was visiting a maximum-security prison and the warden said, "Governor, I got to tell you the prisoners all know you're here. Perhaps, you would like to say a few words." Well, the Governor thought, I can't say my fellow Americans. They're in prison, and I don't know where they're from. I can't say my fellow Republicans (There are none in prison *that's a joke*) can't say my fellow Democrats (that's just not nice and *that is joke*) so finally, Governor Reagan looks at the audience of the prisoners and said, "I am so glad you are here."

Now, listen. I use that opening all the time and I always stop and say after Republican and Democrat that's a joke and my audience kind of chuckles because they know I am not singling out one party or the other. But then I get to the last line and say, "I'm so glad you're here!" Everybody cracks up. Now, remember, I gave attribution. I shake it up just a little bit to make sure my audience is not offended if they're very political-party-specific but it's also a joke, a story that fits most every audience.

Okay, so now you know one of my opening stories. Think about something you've got. I always tell my audience that since I am the youngest of five and the only girl, I've got a lot of stories because I have all brothers. And I do I have a ton of stories and I cycle through them, so the same audience doesn't hear the same one every time I speak. I have the good fortune of being a speaker that gets invited back to the same conference year after year, so I've got to be careful.

I'll tell you something else I have; I have an Excel spreadsheet that has over 1680 quotes. I collect quotes. As I'm reading an article, I keep my Excel spreadsheet open and I do a cut and paste. Why? because I'm a speaker and I need fresh material and I want to be good and current, that's my job and friend you got to do that also since it is your job, and your audience deserves it.

I encourage you to use what you've got to set yourself apart and be memorable. Here's an example of a story I use to connect with my audience. My audiences are surprised to meet a licensed lady auctioneer. Most people have never heard a lady auctioneer chant, but remember going to an auction with a grandparent, so the image of goodwill is implanted in their mind, and this story, my story, sets me apart from most any other speaker they have ever heard. Another reason I offer this story is so many times after a conference, there is one lonely gift basket that no one bid on in the silent auction, so I will offer to sell it by using my auction skills and ten times out of ten, I make them so much money they look around for other items for me to sell. I become invaluable. I am now more memorable, and we all have fun.

The summer after I graduated college, I saw an advertisement that said, "Make a lot of money, become an auctioneer." I immediately thought to myself, *Self, I wanna do this.* When I told my parents of my new endeavor, they said, "Great, Deb. You can pay for it with your own money."

So, I went auctioneers' school. Back then it took about two weeks, and Lo and Behold, I completed the class and was hired by the auction company that had placed the ad, so I learned the business and I had my license. At one time I was the youngest woman in the state of South Carolina who wasn't grandfathered in to hold an auctioneer's license. I stayed with the company a couple of years, had a great time traveling and learning the business from the inside out. Talk about a life-learning experience in dealing with folks I would have never have otherwise met. I like to say that becoming an auctioneer smoothed my uptight prep-school image into someone more congenial and accepting. I will admit I grew tired over time of how some of my buyers "showed out," which is a Southern way of saying some folks' dishonest behavior lessened the joy of the journey for me.

Imagine you're on a stage or the back of a pick-up truck calling bids and you're selling a box lot. A box lot is where you put knickknacks and things that you probably couldn't sell individually, you throw them all in a box and sell it.

Most box lots go for about $5 to $12, so when a box lot hits $20, $30, $40, $50, you got to walk off the stage or hop off the truck and start unloading that box. And you will find the silver candle sticks in the bottom under the towels and then your buyer in the crowd will suddenly disappear, and you must start over with the sale. Happened over and over and over and you know at some point you just get tired of it.

At another auction my job was to start all the State Law Enforcement Division cars - these are the cars that are being sold after a SLED has worn them out. My job was to get up early in the morning, pop the hood, and start the car so I know all forty cars turn over and start. But sure enough when no one is paying attention some good old boy will pull a spark plug or will loosen something so when I go to restart the car it won't start, and they stand around the car they kick the tires and they say well that one won't start and sure enough they buy it for a really great price and then they plug it back in and they drive it off the lot.

Now we're talking years ago so things have changed since then but I can always remember thinking how amazing it was that people spent so much time trying to cheat the system versus doing right the first time because if you did that to a car and we could catch you we would recall the car and we would not let you have it, so you really didn't get away with it and on top of that now we never want you back at our auction again so your two minutes of insanity have now cost you a lifetime of great deals.

Cut out what's unnecessary. Things like my paying for the class isn't all that noteworthy. That I was grandfathered in isn't all that interesting either, and the reason I left the business can be thinned out, so it becomes:

The summer after I graduated college, I saw an advertisement that said, "Make a lot of money, become an auctioneer." So, I went auctioneers' school, and when I completed the class, the company that had placed the ad, hired me.

Imagine you're on a stage or the back of a pick-up truck calling bids and you're selling a box lot. A box lot is where you put knickknacks and things that you probably couldn't sell individually, you throw them all in a box and sell it.

Most box lots go for about $5 to $12, so when a box lot hits $20, $30, $40, $50, you got to walk off the stage or hop off the truck and start unloading that box. And you will find the silver candle sticks in the bottom under the towels and then your buyer in the crowd will suddenly disappear and you must start over with the sale. Happened over and over and over, and you know at some point, you just get tired of it.

Another part of my job was to auction cars being sold after the State Law Enforcement Division had worn them out. My job was to arrive early, pop the hood, and start the engines to be sure all forty cars turned over. But, sure enough, when no one was looking, some good old boy would pull a spark plug or loosen something, so when I went to restart the car, it wouldn't. Now this went one or two ways. A man would either kick the tires or say, "Well, this one won't start." And then, sure enough, they'd buy it for a great price, then plug the spark back in and drive it off the lot.

It's always amazed me when people spend so much time cheating the system versus doing right. the first time because if you did that to a car and we could catch you we would recall the car and we would not let you have it, so you really didn't get away with it and on top of that now we never want you back at our auction again, so your two minutes of insanity have now cost you a lifetime of great deals.

Delivered in a few minutes. Now, I can tell this story fifty times to fifty different audiences, and each time, it'll change ever so slightly, but no matter how the telling shifts, I am able to answer the following questions before I use it.

1. What's the point of the story?
2. Does the story have a beginning, middle, and end?
3. Is the story creative and is it provocative?

What I will be able to say, without a doubt, is my story meets all the guidelines and is a glimpse into who I am beyond my introduction and resume.

WRITE FOR THE EAR, NOT THE EYE

Energy is the lifeblood of a presentation. Energy is what makes you interesting, passionate, easier to understand, natural, and confident. Energy is synonymous with life. Controlled energy may seem quiet on the surface, but it has a strong undercurrent. Without your speaking energy your audience will fill the void with restlessness, and you will lose them. Make sure your voice conveys authority. Think energy, frequency, and vibration.

Over time, you will develop a speaking style that will be easy to understand, listen to, and of course, push your audience into taking the action you need them to take. This "easy-listening" speaking ability takes practice. It takes you thinking about your voice and learning to lower it. Deep breathing helps. The value of your vocal quality and an audience's ability to hear what you say and the power in which you say it. As a speaker it's important that you understand how people hear what your voice is saying to those who are listening to you.

Your voice has an impact on others. You know we judge you on how you look, how you sound, what you say, and your vocal sound says a lot about you.

You and I have heard people speak and our ears hurt – other times we could listen to people speak all day long. Now, why is that? Well, it's vocal quality. A person who speaks in a lower register makes you feel more comfortable and confident due to the deep and rich sound of their voice when that person is speaking. A higher pitched voice tends to be more nasal which many people do not enjoy.

Think about your favorite singers. For a lot of us, we like that lower, soft, sexy voice, that's what makes somebody a star. And yet, occasionally, we hear a soft voice, and that person will also be a star. I'm thinking of Alison Krauss. It's the same thing with Dolly Parton. You can pick either woman out of a crowd because they've developed a sound that's all their own.

I tend to like Peabo Bryson, James Taylor, but then you have somebody like Billy Joel who's a lot like James Taylor, a troubadour and somebody you could listen to all day. Who's your favorite singer? What makes you like them? I am pretty sure you were drawn to the sound of their voice, and that's what I want for you as a speaker.

Now how do you do this? If you have a really high voice, you've got to take a deep strong breath and think about speaking in your lower register, and if you're speaking too low to sound gravelly or older than your years, then you need to lift your voice a bit, so you sound deep and resonant.

Your text needs to be written for the ear and not the eye. The ear can fix what the eye can't see. Your ear is listening for rhythm and cadence and a pleasant sound, so your speech can have dashes, pauses, asides, half sentences, and repetitions, just the way you talk. If this were a perfect English paper it would need to be grammatically correct, but when you speak you have a bit more freedom to use your personality, that's why your speech could have asides or a joke or even use perhaps a half sentence.

Be careful about letting your voice rise at the end of the sentence; this makes it sound like you're asking a question. And don't die out at the end of the sentence; this sounds like you don't believe it yourself.

Think about how a news reporter reads the news. We tend to believe them because they have a vocal rhythm that's comforting to our ears. You have to be extra careful, because you're on a stage and a lot of people are listening and watching and today, they are recording you.

Soft landings and transitions are a standard in the political world, and they are quickly taking hold of the business world. Soft landings and transitions help a speaker turn a question in the direction he or she wants to go. Remember: it's about control, and, as the speaker, you're in control. Soft landings are a way to protect yourself and still get your message across.

Also, these phrases are very polite sounding, but you still get to go where you were going anyway, maintaining your power and choice of direction.

I encourage you to make a copy of this sheet (there's a clean copy in the back of this book) and keep it at your desk so whenever you're on the phone or you must deal with somebody *including your kids* you have the right words to say in the right order at the right time. This sheet gives you a great way to answer anyone and it always puts you in control.

I'm from the South and we pride ourselves on being gracious and kind – now when you get to know us, we're what they call steel magnolias, a woman who possess the strength of steel, yet the gentleness of a magnolia. A magnolia is famous flowering tree – with big white flowers that smell great (primarily seen in the South) so now you know a little southern history – but we get things done the right way and this sheet can help you maintain your authority and power. Let me tell you how it works, pull it out and have it in front of you so we can go through it together.

When people disagree with your position you now have some soft landings to redirect the question or comment. And that is key, redirecting the question or comment. That's the whole point of soft landings and transitions; they help you change the direction of the conversation to put you back in a position of power.

Now you can take any soft landing and pair it to any transition. Let me start for you. "You make it interesting point …. Let me explain …," "I appreciate your position …. Let me add …," "I agree with you ….

79

Equally important ...." Do you see how you can take any soft landing and pair it to any transition?

Now, here's the key. You can never say "but" or "however," if you use a soft landing. Why? because when you use the words "but" or "however," you start a fight. As in, you make it interesting point, but you're a moron. I appreciate your position, however anyone with half a brain .... I agree with you, but you're wrong. I exaggerated these examples. In most cases, you would never call somebody a moron, say they have half a brain, or that they're wrong. At least not right up front but that's what the ear hears, if you say "but" or "however," so you can't say those words with this format. The only time you can use the word "but" is in when you don't have the information handy, so you offer "... *but I can tell you this*." It's almost like you're letting somebody in on a secret, except there is no secret.

Learning how to do soft landings and transition takes time but with practice you can be very good at this, and they'll never see it coming. You can still be very polite and accommodating, but you're still going to go in your direction

I want to share a more sales type of way to overcoming objections. It's very similar to how you make someone feel with soft landings and transitions. It is called the Feel, Felt, Found way. It is a standard sales pitch for business and multi-level marketing that has been around for a while because it works. If you ever attended a sales training course, you would learn this. Here's how it works.

You understand how they feel. Other people have felt the same way. What they found is this .... An example: I know how you feel. I felt the same when I thought about changing. Now I've found that it works better, I have purchased several.

Feel, Felt, Found is a great way to keep you in the game. Fill your arsenal with things that will always keep you in control as a speaker. I've repeatedly said how tough this business is and it is and today's audience, for some reason, think they can say whatever they want but you're not allowed to have a reply. I completely disagree. You have every right to protect yourself. You have every right to set an audience member straight. You have every right to clarify for others who are listening, so when you use soft landings and transitions or something like feel, felt, found, or any other verbal shortcut, friend learn to use it to your best ability. Let it be like a natural conversation because that is the only way to stay one step ahead of an audience member who thinks they should be on the stage and not you.

Being a speaker is like conducting an orchestra. You have the opportunity to point out certain people or instruments, so they can shine. One thing that never fails to happen is when someone stands to ask you a question, they can suddenly feel the spotlight on them, and they bungle the question or comment. Now if someone ask a question and they're good hearted and they stumble, feel free to stop and help them. Maybe they didn't understand something and needed clarification and you can provide that to them and to anyone else who might not have heard your original comments.

It depends on how the question is asked and you get to make a snap judgment then and there on how you are going to respond. If the questioner is hostile, and unfortunately this is happening more and more, I suggest that you let them stand in the light and try to get whatever smart aleck or angry comment they have out because nine times out of ten, they won't be nearly as angry because they stumbled in front of everyone, just let them stand in their light and shine or burn out.

I can remember many years ago I was speaking at a conference. There was an older lady in my audience, who really wanted to be one of the speakers but was not chosen, and somewhere in my presentation I made a statement and she said out loud to everyone around her, "Well, that's not true." I heard her and stopped my presentation and asked her in front of everyone if she knew something different and then I restated my comments to which she replied "Oh, well, I guess I misunderstood."

Now, I'm not sure if she really misunderstood or if she was surprised that I stopped and called her out. All my life I've been very bold because I have had to fight my way to the top. Speaking is a tough business, and in this case, I wasn't going to let somebody question my reputation or allow her jealousy to harm me since I was on the stage, and she wasn't.

Because today's audiences are looking for connection, make sure you save enough time to engage an audience after a talk. Questions after a talk is a way an audience will double check you as a speaker to make sure you were legitimate in your remarks and your content. There is nothing worse than an audience who has waited for you to speak, giving you their time and attention, and when it's over you run out the door to catch your supposed plane. Look at the schedule of the day and make sure that you're on the last flight of the day so you can engage an audience that paid to hear you speak or gave up their time to hear your presentation.

Whether it's due to work pressure or performance exhaustion, I've noticed times when a speaker finishes his or her presentation, it's as if they turn off their brain. They've just given it their all and they want to relax. This respite, and we can wholly blame this on the origination of social media, isn't an option for today's speaker.

To take a breather, your best-case scenario is for your audience to go to another breakout session, because inevitably, depending on the size of the audience, five or ten people will linger back to speak to you directly after speech. They expect your attention. Some go as far to presume a personal connection. As a speaker, that's how you know you leave a solid impression. I often remind speakers that when someone accepts an invitation to speak, they are the captain of the ship and the shepherd of the flock. A captain doesn't leave the ship, nor does a shepherd leave even a single lamb behind. Stay until the end.

This isn't to say there aren't speaking engagements where I'm tired from traveling, or somehow, I missed lunch, but learning to love your audience is something that happens over time. A speaker has an unofficial contract with the audience. It is the speaker's job to fulfill the contract, even when it's inconvenient.

STAGE READY TIPS

I wouldn't worry so much about the timing of yesterday's setbacks or holdups. I'd worry more about social media. I've witnessed content creators leap to tenuous success. Social media has changed how we introduce ourselves and, ultimately, how we interact with a world audience. For some, it's a terrific tool, and for others, it'll be the weapon. The reason I am urging you on this issue of time is to get going now, the wild swings of our current culture will make or break you when the pendulum swings the other way. What was acceptable even a few years ago most likely will get you ripped to shreds in the weaponization of social media today where unknown faces hiding behind keyboards are the judge and jury.

Social media has changed the way speakers are viewed these days. One wrong word or gesture and you will be apologizing for something you didn't mean to say or do or has no meaning to you or your life changing message but by your presence and by being out front will at some point outrage some lone actor with nothing to do and no real interest in truth or facts will launch an attack. Today the court of public opinion is always in session and as speakers on the stage we must be careful that our defense, our message, and our meaning is strong and sure and is backed up with facts that cannot honestly and fairly be disputed.

Writer and social commentator Joel Lee says this: "Social media users, everyday people like you and me have a tremendous amount of power today and when that power is combined with the pervasive growth of outrage culture, social media becomes a destructive force that can ruin innocent lives."

I am not trying to scare you off the stage. Be reminded there's a difference between time and timing. What might be funny tomorrow, won't necessarily be what's in good taste next week, and when you put yourself out there, you will be trolled.

You need to be strong in the light you give to help others on their way with a lighted path. You must do the work to be amazing, there are no shortcuts anymore. You're not responsible for how people treat you. But you must be strong enough to keep going no matter what is thrown your way.

As a speaker when you approach the lectern, many times a computer from the previous speaker will already be there, so where do you put your notes? Do you close the computer so you can put your notes on top? do you ask someone if they can move it to the side? if you turn the computer off will it mess up the whole background or the flow of the event after your speaking time is finished? You must think about these silly little annoyances before you come to the stage or the lectern.

If your presentation has sound, do you know which cord plugs into your PC or MAC? Otherwise, you'll be holding a microphone right next to your computer so the audience can hear the clip that you're playing. All this must be done before you ever arrive and if you do it on the fly make sure you've got some good lines to get you through so the audience does not become annoyed as you're clearing off a space for you to present.

THE OLD SPOTLIGHT EFFECT

Above all the most important thing is that you are open friendly, encouraging, and powerful. Remember these people have paid for you to be rock-star amazing. That's why you can't go drinking the night before or binge watch Netflix until 2:00 in the morning. In the morning, consider not watching hours of the news and seeing the horrors of the world. Yes, you need to know what is going on in the world but remember your job is to change the lives of those who have come to listen to you speak, friend think about what you put in your mind before you step on a stage and my advice is what you put in your mind is your message, why you're giving it, and what outcome you hope to have and then fill your lungs with air an energy and let's go.

Something I do when I get up in the morning, I will go have my breakfast, I'll come back to the hotel room, brush my teeth, and make sure I'm ready to go for the day and then I pause and take a little bit of quiet time to think about who I'm speaking to, what my topic is, what three words or big messages I want them to remember from our time together. Please don't go rushing to your engagement without a pause to gather yourself, you need to be of sound mind and body to perform.

Remember when I said in the very beginning that when people come to hear you speak nobody is hoping you're awful. Remember I said that everyone is cheering for you and hoping you're amazing because they are the ones who have to listen to you? They choose to listen to you, so with that in mind, I want to describe a trick your mind has a tendency to play on you.

We've covered what it means to be in the spotlight, but there's something called the Spotlight Effect, and it's an overestimation about how you, the speaker, thinks everyone is looking at you, judging you, and grading you. The truth is, if you're on stage, there likely is a spotlight right on you but don't confuse this with the Spotlight Effect. Yes, your audience is looking at you. Obviously, they came to hear you speak. The distinction is your audience is primarily focused on your message.

The term "spotlight effect" originated in research by Gilovich, Medvec, and Savitsky, where they commented that "People tend to believe that the social spotlight shines more brightly on them than it really does." And then our brains — because we live in our own little world and think we are the center of the universe — wrongly assume every action we take, every word we speak, every movement we make is being judged, but it isn't.

Have you ever noticed when you spill coffee or something on your shirt, and for the rest of the day, you think about it and try to cover it up, but most people never see the stain? The idea that everyone is looking at the stain on your shirt is all in your head. That's the spotlight effect. It's a term social psychologists use to convey those humans tend to highlight their flaws, but it's egocentric.

They say the spotlight affect is brightest when people aren't comfortable with their physical appearance. I've spoken about this before, but friend, your audience really never looks at you, not really. The person standing at the front wearing a blue suit with a white shirt and a red tie or a nice black dress with a scarf isn't why the audience has come. They came to hear your message. They're intent on hearing your message. You're just the messenger. Sure, people are paying attention to you, but it isn't as if they're zeroing in on your shortcomings or weak spots.

Now, it's true that as a presenter you are always on display. So, of course, be careful on how you dress and your grooming, but rest assured, you may experience biasness no matter what you do. Do you remember a guy named Jeffrey Gitomer? Now this was several years ago, but he became famous for his *Little Red Book of Selling*, and in every photo, he had of himself — even though he was a white-collar professional — he wore a shirt with a name patch branded "Jeffrey."

This brand became so popular that some speakers stopped wearing suits on stage and would copy his look by wearing a basic work shirt with the name patch. He changed the industry forever, and that was his brand. And it worked for him. He was no longer the "stuffy guy in a suit and tie" that made learning how to sell to others hard. He made it easy, and he made it fun. He was laid back. In fact, he totally changed a very staid industry into something that anybody could do, and he became very successful at it. His books are still available today.

While you don't see him on the circuit anymore, he's made his money and gave others the chance to dress down and still be successful. Sorry to say my brand isn't as clever, but it is just as well thought out. I tend to wear navy or black pants and jacket with a colorful shirt. I've had two knee replacements, so pants are much more comfortable for me than wearing a dress or a skirt, it's a fine line because as a lady I still need to be seen as feminine, but I need to be comfortable because I tend to walk and talk and move as I'm explaining and training and teaching people how to be good on a stage or be a better speaker or how to survive a press conference. What's your brand? Have you thought about it?

When it comes to clothing, I'm often asked these basic questions – should I dress better than my audience? do I dress to stand out? or do I dress casually? can I be overdressed? Or can I wear my standard uniform... let me answer these questions as I talk about clothing for men and women. I think that you should dress at (or just above) the same level as your audience and I will add that you should dress in a manner that makes you comfortable and puts you on a level that says you're a professional.

Once you start talking because you are so good, they won't be noticing what you are wearing anyway.

Now if you know everybody is going to be in golf shirts and blue jeans or cowboy boots and hats don't show up in a tuxedo – you dress in the manner that's appropriate for the audience that you will be speaking to... come on you know this.

Let me just remind you that your clothing tells the audience a little bit about you, so for some of you, you need to spend some money and clean up your wardrobe.

Most stages are not carpeted so if you have hard soled shoes, I will hear you walk on the stage – I like that sound if you are showing power and strength keep to the hard soled shoes... if your talk is more lighthearted and it's not life-changing per se you can go with soft soled shoes. I encourage all my clients to go with a hard sole – I want people to hear that you are serious you mean business and you're not going to slink away. Obviously, this is up to you but remember to maintain a powerful present I need to hear your power.

Oh, and by the way your shoes must be polished and clean... ladies the heels on your shoes have to be clean and not scuffed up. We judge people by their shoes you can have fun footwear but make sure they are well taken care of.

I'm often asked about jewelry. If your jewelry is real, I say wear it. Bling it up; it lets the audience know you're successful. I would rather your jewelry be of excellent quality and understated then cheap and overstated, but that's me. You do what's best for where you are and what your personality is.

These are some generalizations, Ladies, nine out of ten times, you will be handed a Lavaliere microphone, which has a clip on it, so you will need to clip the mic to your clothing somewhere, meaning you either need a pocket or a waistband or they're going to have to tape it to your back or adhere it to your bra strap. Think about this when you dress to speak.

You might wear muted lipstick shades day to day, but when you're under a camera's light, add something that pops, maybe even some eyeliner and blush to your cheeks, elements that serve to enhance or accentuate your face.

The good news is you can change it up occasionally, but as your coach I'm going to tell you to find a look and stick with it if you plan to "brand your look."

The speaking industry is interesting when you realize the top speakers tend to either look alike or there's a one or two individuals out there that have created their own look. For years I was a member of the National Speakers Association, for what I teach I really don't need them, but it was a good learning experience for me to be surrounded by people who were in hopes of being the next big thing. What I found fascinating was that, although everyone claimed to have a unique message, they all looked and sounded exactly alike.

When I speak, I am on a stage, sometimes I speak from one to three to six hours. That's a long time to be speaking and as a woman who's getting a little up there in age standing that long in high heels just doesn't suit me and of course with two new knees it's not really possible, and I will say that is a lot of stress on the body and as you get older you're going to need to make some changes that accommodate the pressure of being on a stage that long – whether it's compression socks, or knowing how much water you can drink to keep you hydrated without having to leave the stage to go to the bathroom or are you able to miss a meal without getting ill? You need to think through these situations because sometimes as a speaker you're either crunched in before somebody, who just happened to show up who's an elected official and they demand to be heard or the speaker before you, who ran late, and now your time has been cut in half, how are you going to show up?

The speaking industry is a little more casual today than it used to be, different speakers are defining their look i.e. Tony Robbins looks great in a suit but he also tends to wear jeans and a shirt, kind of like when we were kids your pastor always wore a suit to church and now at some of these churches the guys and gals in the front tend to look like they just walked out of a grocery store.

So, what's your look? What's your color? For a long time the speaking industry pushed women to wear a scarf or a brooches or pin to add a defined look, they told guys to wear cufflinks, suspenders, and bow ties... remember the starched shirt you used to have to wear to show that you were a successful person and not an easy wash and wear shirt that might have a wrinkle or two or heaven forbid a shirt that was not tucked in. Can you remember the shirts that had a different colored collar than the shirt, there's still a few guys on the circuit still dressing like they did back in their mafia Corleone days, or how about the look that Regis Philbin made popular where the shirt and tie looked just alike against a different color jacket the boring monochrome look. Thank goodness that went away. And if you're still wearing that look just know you are now one in a million... which might be your brand.

I won't spend a lot of time on clothing, because we all live in different parts of the country and world, and dress requirements are different for everybody according to their job. That being said, there are a few rules that will never go out of style here they are.

Personal strength can also be perceived by clothing. Here are a few tips:

- Your clothes should not be more interesting than you are.
- They should fit well and be neat and clean.
- Choose clothes that fit in with the level you want to influence.

In other words, dress the part and remember that the medium is often more important than the message. How you look is crucial, as perception often becomes reality.

Now, if I'm being honest, those among us who are lucky enough they can wear the same blue suit all week and only change their socks and tie and be deemed presentable have it easy.

Our clothes tell our colleagues what we're all about. Do you want others to think you're a plodder ...creative ... gregarious ...secure... conservative ...timid...self-conscious? Your wardrobe has the power to convey all these messages, so make it an asset...not a detriment.

Make your clothes boldly convey I am suited up. I am ready to play. I am wearing the appropriate uniform to achieve my goal.

Clothing telegraphs to the world not just who you think you are, but who you want to be. You've heard the old joke: If you don't think little things make a difference – try going to bed with a mosquito.

Let's go over a few things you should do and have when you're traveling to a speaking engagement.

- ✓ Pack an extra shirt and an extra outfit just in case.
- ✓ Be really careful to make sure you always have identification on you in case you need to get into a building, or somebody asks for it, not just for the airport but for the conference center as well.
- ✓ Carry a hard copy of your speech and one on a thumb drive. Do the same thing with any handouts and your introduction.

It's amazing how many times you get to a conference, and someone forgot to print your handouts and introduction.

✓ Get a good night's rest and do not drink alcohol the night before or, at the very least, limit your consumption.

✓ Always ask for a glass, and don't say, "Let me take a sip of water" or something silly, just take a drink. And make sure you drink enough water, so you're not dehydrated when you begin to speak. Don't worry about having to go to the bathroom; go to the bathroom before you begin speaking and since you normally speak for twenty, maybe forty minutes, you should be fine bathroom-wise but drink plenty of water in the morning to hydrate your system, because you will sweat it out as you're speaking.

✓ For those of you who truly suffer anxiety, not those who are nervous but truly have an issue with anxiety, ask your doctor for something called a beta-blocker; beta-blockers calm the body down so you should feel calmer when you speak. Now, I don't recommend it, but as your coach, you need to know you have some options. And don't take this the first time you speak; you need to take it in advance and see how it affects you.

✓ On the morning you speak, you might not be hungry but eat something, even if it's a protein bar or a banana; you need something in your system besides coffee.

✓ I always keep an extra mint in my pocket so when I'm done speaking and folks came up to me afterward, I have fresh breath. There's nothing worse than bad breath after you speak for a while.

Since most of you reading this book are speakers, let me quickly address that if you happen to be a singer or if you are a guest of somebody on a stage, the assumption you understand how acoustics work in a building and your team, assuming you've got one, knows how to use the stage for your best appearance. Most of you will be spotlighted if you are giving a reading or if you are doing a one-act play and that's a part of your presentation, realize that using the stage to your advantage is only going to enhance the audience enjoyment of the experience because you've mastered the stage presence, the lighting, the curtains, the sound, the way the furniture is placed.

Always be aware that there are probably ten or more cables on the floor, knowing how you're going to and from the stage that's one level, so you literally walk on and off the stage or do you come up steps onto the stage? If it's a boardroom and you're seated on the side, how do you wrestle yourself to the front of the room to make a presentation without stepping over briefcases, boxes, and oversized chairs and add to that many times a screen will be behind you, have you done the work in advance to set it up for your success? Seriously, no one else is going to do it for you, so be early and be prepared to make it work.

Ideally you have a handler but most of you on the circuit will need to be prepared to handle your own presentation and stage setup because you know how it should be seen, heard, felt, and experienced.

Platform awareness is also from the perspective of an audience member looking towards you the speaker in front. Is there something in their way? I can remember thinking I got great tickets for a rodeo only to find out there was a post in the way, and I kept having to duck around it to see the cowboy get bucked off; no wonder the tickets were so cheap.

I will never forget, I was at a conference and the keynote speaker was someone I had never heard of, and I doubt anybody else had, nor will you see him speak at any other conference due to his disrespect of his audience. As I was sitting with a friend of mine in the audience, he walked to the front and began his talk and a few minutes into his talk, he started walking. He walked to the left side of the stage and came down the steps, he walked down the side of the room, so the cameraman was literally having to follow him walking all over the room.

Now as an audience member sitting there it was hard to turn your head to the left and the right and to the back of the room and then he came up the aisle to the front and down the aisle to the back and around the aisle up the other side. Now, I know in his mind he thought "I'll keep people focused on me because I'm walking." But the audience reaction was much different. The audience was annoyed, and after a while, it almost became silly. It was so obvious either he had forgotten to take his ADD medicine, or his message was so thin, he disguised it by his ridiculous antics.

It was a cheap speaker ploy and after a while the cameraman gave up and did a wide room shot of the traveling speaker, so he never had great close-ups to use for any other purpose. The speaker also lost his audiences' attention because we could not follow him or his message. To this day I don't know who he was, and I know he's never been invited back because I speak at that conference now and my friends laugh about the silly "walking, talking, traveling speaker."

So, platform awareness comes in different aspects. As the speaker you must know how you're getting on and how you're getting off the stage. I've written many times about falling off a stage. You know many times the steps that go up to a stage are portable, so they're not very sturdy. This one time I thought I would be clever to walk down a couple steps and make notes on a white board only to have my feet slip out from under me. Down I went. I had to pop up and keep going, of course the group that hired me wondered if I was going to sue, and the 900 people in the audience wanted to know if I was going to finish my talk. Yes, things happen. You just keep going. In this case, I had another hour and a half to speak. It was brutal. However, the show went on. As they say, the show must always go on. Even when it's tough, even when things go sideways, it's your production; it's your show.

PART III

PERFECTING YOUR PLATFORM

6

PERSEVERANCE

I always encourage my speaking clients to do whatever it takes to get into the room before it fills with your audience so you can look around. Many times when I arrive at my hotel I'll ask at the front desk where I will be speaking, what room will I be in the next day, and if there's no one in the room I will walk around the stage so I get my bearings, most every time I say a prayer over the room to make sure my message is heard in the right way, I really focus on how to get on and off the stage (remember I've fallen a few times I really try not to do that anymore) so from a purely practical perspective I learn my stage. I learn my platform. I know where I'm going to walk, I know how many steps to get on the stage and get off the stage, I know how many steps I can take to the front and back of the stage. I set myself up for success beforehand. Sometimes, if I'm not at the hotel the day before I will try to slip in and hear the speaker before me and watch how they're handling the stage and how the audience is paying attention. I like to see where the sound desk is and how bright the lights shine as I am getting to and from the stage. I do my homework in advance. It would be silly for me (and you) not to take advantage of every opportunity to be amazing when it is so readily available.

CRITIQUE YOUR SPEAK

As much as I want you to believe in yourself, I want you to be open to criticism. At some point all speakers need to critique their speech from an outsider perspective. The reason you do this is that you want to make sure all your hard work hits the mark, reaches its point, rings a bell, touches a chord.

Pretty much after every presentation I ask someone I trust, "How did I do?" Believe it or not I'm not looking for someone to say I was amazing, I worked hard enough to be amazing, but what I really want to know is did my message reach my audience? After a presentation when I'm in my hotel room or headed to the airport I like to think through a quick checklist of my talk so I know that I've done what I had planned to do and can be prepared for next time.

- ✓ Was I satisfied with the whole of my presentation?
- ✓ Did I feel confident, powerful, and assured?
- ✓ Was the audience with me or did I lose some of them and why/when?
- ✓ How long was the applause *not that that matters* but it lets me know that they appreciate my work. Did I get a standing ovation or were they bolting for the door to get to lunch?
- ✓ How was my delivery? Did I mess up any words if so which ones and why?
- ✓ Did I go over or under my time?
- ✓ Was the event what I expected in regard to audience size, introduction, mic, location?

I will sit down and go through this checklist to make sure I have accomplished what I should, and that I am better for next time. Then I will recall how I saw my audience from the stage... why do I do this – because I want to get better every time, I stand to speak...

So, I'll recall if at any time my audience looked confused? was there a point in my speech where they were nodding their head in agreement? did I ever see someone who looked bored or who spent their time talking to the neighbor or furiously writing notes... I gather this intel for my next talk.

If I noticed at a certain place in my talk where folks looked confused than I need to see if I need to change something in my speech... when I notice that they were nodding in agreement that I know that part of the speech really resonated with them. If I could pinpoint a time, they look bored – then I need to fix something in my speech and if they were furiously taking notes than I should probably give a better handout or put different words on my slides. Reading the room. Simply learning to read your audience will make you a better more memorable speaker.

WRITER'S BLOCK

It is bound to happen, you are so excited about your topic, you know you're going to do well, you know the audience and their expectations for your talk, and you sit down to write your outline or put your scattergram together and then nothing comes.

You see, writer's block happens to the best of us... all that energy and excitement suddenly just seems to drain away into a big black hole, but it can't... You have a job to do, you cannot wallow in your confusion, it's time to go to work and sometimes you have to push yourself even if you don't feel like it, that's why you have deadlines, that's why we practice, that's why we write our speech out, we leave nothing to chance – we set ourselves up for success.

Writer's block is simply a mental pause because you're tangled up with worry about the big ending, the whole speech, and not taking it piece by piece, while I can appreciate you wanting to be perfect, remember this is a first draft work session and you have to treat it as such, so don't let your ego get in the way of doing the work – when you haven't even started the process. The best thing to do is just sit down and force yourself to start writing. That's why I encourage a scattergram, just write down anything and everything that pertains to what you want to talk about and sometimes on my page I make very clear things I will not talk about in this talk, so we don't get off track. A scattergram is for you alone, it sets you up for success, everything you think about on this topic you write it down, so you leave nothing out. Will you use it all? Probably not, but at least it's there. One thing I have found is the questions I had put on my scattergram sometimes are the questions my audience has, and I was already set with an answer because I had done the work.

I always encourage my clients who get stuck to go outside for a walk – a walk is a great idea if you have writer's block, and you feel that you're stuck – that extra air and oxygen will help you as you think through your talk as you walk.

I have also found that by putting things in order like making your bed or cleaning up your car or the house or doing the laundry or dishes... by putting things in order in your world, many times will help put order in your mind. It will help push through any limiting belief you may have because if you can do something small you can do something big.

So go ahead and take a walk, a nap, a moment for reflection can really help your mind settle into the proper organization of your talk. It's ok to let your speech rest a while, or go out to dinner, or for ice cream, wash your car, take a nap but don't let it sit too long.

The best way to beat writer's block is to start writing everything you have about the topic that you think you would like to talk about, put it on paper, it could be a rough outline or in bullet point format, it doesn't have to be perfect. This is a work session you can refine it later.

But just stopping because you've got "writer's block" is not going to work and your speech won't get done and then you won't have time to practice. Then you'll stand up and rush through something that is not your best work and the opportunity you had to change your life and the lives of those who came to hear you speak will be completely gone.

The number one issue when it comes to writer's block as you think it has to be perfect the first time. It doesn't. A good speech will have three or four outlines, you'll make changes, you'll move things around, that's why you have to start early and give yourself plenty of time, writing a speech the night before is a waste of your effort and your audience's time, you're better than that don't do it. Don't get so caught up in perfect slides in perfect music and perfect outlines, writer's block will untangle itself when you give it time and space and you must do the work.

I know a lot of my speaker friends will write a draft set it aside and come back to it a couple of times because in the back of their mind, knowing they have a big deal event coming up, that speech will start to take form in their mind. There's nothing wrong with taking a break in fact your mind might need that so your brain can untangle the thoughts you have for your speech.

EFFECTIVE MANAGEMENT

To maintain a lifetime career in speaking isn't easy. Gone are the days of Zig Ziglar, Jim Rohn, Bob Proctor, Les Brown, and to a certain extent, Tony Robbins. They started young, built strong careers, and were able to maintain it. Each had the mental fortitude to get up and do the work every day, and it's worth pointing out that they were all lifelong learners. Even when they started to make money, they created new content, but in many ways the old guard had it much, much easier than we do today.

Back then all they had were cassette tapes, real stage events, and books to sell in the back of the room. There were no overnight successes, they worked at it year after year after year. Again, I'm talking about the fathers of the self-help movement. It's where I studied. Those were the folks who put it on paper, said it from the stage, created audio files, and taught others to be successful with useful road maps to success that worked.

America was different back then. They were byproducts of the Greatest Generation. All they thought about was getting ahead and bringing others along with them. They knew opportunity was created by hard work; work they were willing to do because they weren't going back to the farm.

Back then there was no Silicon Valley. There were few titans of industry. There weren't iPhones. They weren't on the cover of magazines. No, these men and a few women spoke in order to change the world. They used their know-how to make a difference. Simpler times created greater opportunity, because unlike today, the world wasn't so full of hucksters, peddlers, and late-night hawkers.

It is rare to find those type of speakers nowadays, where social media can make an unknown person famous for a week or break a well-known speaker within the hour. I believe we also suffer today with people believing their feelings are their life, not something that can be changed according to how they feel. If it's a feeling, it's not a real deep issue. You hurt me goes to cancel culture. There, there, there: there's no foundation, no knowledge, and no learning.

Speakers back in the good old days wouldn't have put up with the self-important, self-indulgent children who seem to run the world. They had rules back then. You dressed a certain way, you spoke a certain way, and you never swore from the stage, because there was a certain decorum of what was acceptable. No one took pride in being uneducated, so they learned on their own. They never thought they were the smartest people in the room; they came into the room to learn something new for the next event they would create. They were grounded in what they knew worked, because theirs was a hardscrabble life that gave them insight to build a world for others without making the same mistakes.

Recently, I looked up a current list of famous self-help speakers. Yossi Ghinsberg, Ken Blanchard, Joe Simpson, Chris Widener, Steve Pavlina, Aron Ralston, Eric Bailey, Joe Vitale, Carrie Prejean, Edward Liddy, Caroline Kennedy, Tiger Woods, Roger Clemens, Jill Abramson, David Bach, Valorie Burton, and Michael Bernard Beckwith. It was interesting how short many of those careers were, but their names were still on the list. They certainly didn't go down in history as somebody to follow, because their training is no longer valuable in today's marketplace, true the marketplace has changed, but their message was only valuable for a short time. So, while a speaking career is rewarding, if you're not careful, you'll have a short shelf life. I encourage you to keep up with the times, be forward-thinking in your mindset, find ways to get your message out there so you can find audiences who need to hear from you.

Ultimately, what I've learned is you become a good speaker once you've walked a mile in the worn-out shoes that got you to a stage.

I mentioned him earlier. I have probably listened to every Jim Rohn story that's out there, I know about his life as a young man, about meeting the person that changed his life, how he learned because he listened, and then he put into action what he did. I know his life story because he repeats parts of it throughout every talk he gives, while that works for him that may not work for you. I think you become a good speaker, one that people want to listen to when you've put in the work that made the difference in your life. Some of the highest paid speakers are sports figures, they probably don't start most of their speeches by telling you how much money they make, what most of them tell you is where they came from, how hard it was, how they had no expectation, how they were going to get out of where they were no matter what it took. Well, for some of them that is storytelling. They have inflated their story for the interest of their audience, for others that's their life and they told it as it was, not sanitized, not pretty, not bombastic, but simply as a speaker on a stage. As a speaker, you get to choose what you're going to say.

I know a lot of speaking books like to talk about storytelling, I'm a little bit hesitant because I want your stories to be true, I want your stories to have impact, I don't want you to weave a story because you think it's clever. Your audience can tell a difference, what matters is what part of your story changed your life and only you can tell us that. And what makes that so valuable is that others cannot take it from you and if they have any common sense, they won't copy you because those are your hardscrabble life stories. Those are the stories that make storytelling worthwhile. I've talked before about the pendulum that swings back and forth when it comes to storytelling it goes in and out of vogue, the problem is with most stories they're not true, they have no meaning, they have no real adherence to the topic at hand, they were a quick story made up to add interest, to try to be funny, to try to pat your own self on the back in front of an audience that (trust me) can tell the difference, so while we don't get hung up on storytelling we all have crafted or you should be crafting the stories of your life, from when you were young, the lessons learned, the heartbreak, the success, joy, failure, anything that molded you into being who you are today. Now that's a story worth telling.

You may be wondering once you're in the spotlight, how much can you control? I believe as a speaker you can control as much as you want once you're on the stage under the bright hot spotlight. I've had speakers get so choked up they could not continue their message, so they turned the house lights up, everyone took a break, they walked off, they came back, and they started again. I've had speakers ask audience members to please be quiet (doesn't go over well) but sometimes you have to. I've had speakers mock their audience (that's not good). I have found the reason most speakers lose their cool on a stage just because they're exhausted or the audience knows more than they do, and they got caught, so fear, fight, flight, is what prompted them to not be the best that they could be. You can control the stage, you can control the spotlight, only if you have something to say.

One thing that hasn't change is that each of these individuals gave their audiences what they needed, and they trusted the experience enough so that they came back for more.

The internet is a worldwide platform that gives even the littlest guy a chance. And while that opportunity is wonderful, and it has leveled the playing field seriously look and see who has been around and has stayed relevant if their only platform had been social media, no book, no podcast, no stage, no TV appearances, no radio interviews. This is a business that is built on steps and the first step is to have something to say, the second is to find an audience, and the third is where you find your stage.

For a couple of years, I followed a guy who I really liked by the name of Casey Neistat, he's done some amazing work on commercials for Nike but because the Internet is all consuming 24/7 Casey appears to have burnt out, he moved from New York City to California, he doesn't post much anymore, where he was posting every single day, now he's putting time into building his health and his family. He had success no doubt, but I miss him because in my opinion he was a true-blue entrepreneur with big ideas that not only won but beat the marketplace. That being said the system of cranking out social media to stay relevant is really hard to do without paying a team to keep you in the spotlight and that takes a boatload of cash, so unless you win the lottery let me encourage you to do it the old-fashioned way. Have something to say, find an audience who wants to hear it and willing to pay and learn from you and then find your stage.

With platforms, like TikTok and YouTube famous with no time invested, notoriety though often tedious and time-consuming, social media is free to everyone to absolutely anyone willing to put in the time and effort.

It allows for:

1. Brand curation
2. Brand advocacy
3. Becoming a go-to industry expert
4. Interactive exchanges

I can honestly tell you that when I do research or study or look for new information on public speaking, how to deal with the media and crisis communication, it's almost like a vacation for me because I love to learn, and I love to know what's new in the ever-changing marketplace. I want my clients to be up to date on the latest issues that will protect them on and off the stage. Since coaching is such a large part of my business, I have to constantly keep up to protect them, their company, and their reputation. My lifelong learning enthusiasm I believe, keeps me relevant in the marketplace and thus I have staying power.

A while back I was cleaning out my office and I came across a file of speeches I no longer give, it was so strange to go back and read them and although they are very good, they're not relevant today. I did the work, but that's not how the world works and because the world changed, I had to change with it. Who knows when and if the pendulum will swing back and those talks will be relevant again? I will be ready, with some updating no doubt!

Staying power is something all speakers need to strive for if you plan to stay in this business, you have to be relevant, you have to be up to date, you have to be current, most importantly you have to be excited and exciting to listen to. Learn to read your audience, learn to work with those who hire you, do things out of the ordinary, write that book you keep talking about, do the online class you promised you would do, start your blog, put yourself out there in such a way that the world can't imagine not interacting with you. Then you'll have staying power.

I know instinctively you are not a jerk; jerks don't read books or do online work to make themselves better. No, jerks think they know it all. By the simple fact of you picking up a book to make sure that you are doing all you know to do to be Rockstar amazing tells me that you're pretty remarkable, that being said I will tell you it is sometimes very hard not to slay a smart-aleck audience member.

There's no doubt that you're probably pretty quick with a good comeback, a funny line, a great comment, or story but there is a fine line between what is funny and what is not with an audience. A line you might have used in the past, which made the audience laugh out loud holding their sides having a hard time breathing because you were so hysterical, might make the next audience look at you like you have two heads and a tail. I have the good fortune of being pretty quick on my feet, I'm the youngest of five, all brothers, I had to learn quickly to defend myself, I am well read and I fill in on a local talk radio station, where every caller seems to have mean, hateful, snarky comments so I've gotten pretty good at my comebacks, but I have found many times as a stage speaker I need to keep my snarky, witty, impressive, clever, outstanding, hysterical, well-worded comments to myself when dealing with a live audience. Why? Because if we're not careful, that quick retort or response will absolutely slay an audience member and publicly embarrass them for all to see. I know it's not fair, that they can be mean and hateful but speaker you cannot. Now, you might have intended your remark to put the audience member in their place, to maintain control or simply to quiet them so you can move on but if you are not careful with your witty comment or clever saying or amazing comeback you leader, speaker, rock star, in an odd sense, you attacked an audience member, and then others will wonder why you, speaker, were such a jerk.

As a speaker, one of my newer topics is crisis communications.

Something I would have never considered as a part of my offerings when I started out, in this new environment, though I can give you all the words to speak and sound amazing for you and your company, when the canons start firing and your team starts to run, if you don't know how to rally your forces back in order to protect your team or yourself, I'll have felt I had done a disservice, so in addition to teaching public speaking for the professional and how to deal with the media, I retooled some of my materials to craft a talk about what it takes to survive not only in a crisis but also with every audience you touch.

The key to survival in today's cancel culture is being able to have a clear, concise, and consistent message that conveys empathy, compassion, and humanness to connect with your audience. Let me repeat that: There is nothing more important as a speaker than to craft clear, concise, and consistent content that conveys empathy, compassion, and humanness towards any issue at hand. Without these emotions and realities, you will not be heard above the noise, and you might very well be cancelled if you don't live out the values you claim you live by.

As a speaker who has been blessed to survive the hot mess the national speaking circuit has become, more and more, I see colleagues on the sideline hawking books and seminars and online classes and whatever else they can rope others into buying, but unfortunately because they are out of date, their ideas no longer serve or are relevant in the current marketplace.

I have the good fortune to train the next generation of political leaders at campaign schools across the country. There's a former trainer, whose message didn't keep up with the times and her book is so out of date, the information isn't useful in this generation and how things are accomplished on the campaign trail. Recently, she offered her books for free. Even then, there were no takers. No one took them. They have no value. She was desperate to use the "gift" to create a post about how the campaign school was using her materials, but it all fell short when no one wanted them and wouldn't pay the postage for the "free" books. As a speaker, because of the world we live in and the explosive growth of online media if you do not keep up, you and your message will be left behind. You must do the work to be relevant.

I cannot begin to tell you how many of my speeches I mothballed because the world had changed and although the information was good and, in many cases, relevant, they aren't amazing enough for me to use.

I'm sure you've seen this, and I mentioned this earlier, a speaker on the circuit was very overweight and his shtick was to open with a litany of jokes about his size. Due to health concerns, he worked hard and lost a massive amount of weight. Unfortunately, he still starts every talk with when he was overweight. Watching his audience, I noticed not only did no one laugh but also the look of confusion for those who didn't know his story was one of disgust. Not only was his timing off, but he also refused to "step into his today" and retool his message for those waiting to be inspired, directed, and encouraged.

What was funny yesterday won't necessarily cut it today. You see and hear it with speakers across the country. From the former beauty queens who regale the audience with once-upon-a-time stories to the singer who can't hit the notes and lets the music pull him over the finish line. Don't be that speaker. Figure it out, update your message, understand what today's audiences want and need. That's the gig.

No matter how self-confident, how whole-pie confident, or how high you've set your confidence switch, if you're unprepared or ill-prepared, no amount of quick wit, good looks, or mindless chatter will save you once you're on stage or have gone live in front of a rolling camera.

Humor will always serve you well, but when someone fails to "stand and deliver," more often than not, it's because they failed to prepare.

You cannot crack a few jokes, offer a few good quotes, rattle off a few statistics, and throw a few slides on a screen and be successful. You are not Google; you have to know your topic. You have to know it inside and out. You need to sit yourself down and anticipate questions. You have to practice what you're going to say, and then practice again and again.

Nowadays, with social media, everything you say and do is recorded somewhere and, with that in mind, as a speaker, you need to know whatever content you intentionally or unwittingly create will likely be repeated, so make sure you're repeatable. Make certain your words won't unintentionally become buffooned sound bites or a meme that haunts you for life.

Remember the ten-year rule, give or take. The world's most trusted social researcher Malcolm Gladwell says it takes around 10,000 hours to become a master at something. So, just because you haven't booked that $10K speaking engagement doesn't mean you should chuck it all and throw in the towel. Everyone gets frustrated by the business. Everyone hears their shares of nos. We're stereo-typed. Event organizers don't always call back.

"EVOLVE AND PIVOT" MAKE PROGRESS

In my family there was never a distinction between my brothers' abilities and mine. I was taught to be self-sufficient, forward-thinking, and have boundless energy, because that's what my brothers had, and if I planned to survive in a male-dominant, four-son household, I had to learn to run with wolves. As far as gender roles and stereotypes go, my parents weren't having it. They never made a distinction or gave leniency or made excuses, as far as I could tell, and never gave it much thought that I was a girl. And I was in the fray. I was taught to play baseball and football along with all the other sports.

Now, when we were little, every summer we would go to Isle of Palms for two weeks. Let me slow things down a minute. When my mom married my stepdad, my brother David and I inherited three blond-haired, blue-eyed brothers. They were a good bit older than me, so they spent a good bit of their vacation trying to lose their little sister. Because I was small and not a great swimmer all I ever got to do was pick up shells and wait for the Charlie Chip truck to deliver our weekly ration of potato chips. Sometimes Dad would force them to take me fishing from the bridge or crabbing off the shore, but mostly I wandered up and down the beach looking for them.

To be clear, it always took me about a week to figure out my brothers didn't want me tagging along with them, but usually, the second week of vacation was better. My mom would convince me that she and my dad would be fun on the beach, so I could just hang out with them, still picking up sand dollars, shells, and starfish.

The second week of vacation was always the same. Since David and I tanned easily, we turned golden brown, whereas my stepbrothers turned beet red. They'd be so burnt they couldn't go out during the day, and I got the job of spraying them down with Solarcaine, and since they couldn't go outside, they played card games with me. I would trade aloe sprays for games of cards, unless, of course, I lost, in which case, in a clear reversal of events, they would have to come find me. But, hey, it was progress.

It's also a great lesson on pivoting.

KEEP CALM AND DON'T FEED THE TROLLS

If you've been in the business any amount of time, you undoubtedly consider it a privilege that somebody offers you an opportunity to speak from the stage on a topic you love and know something about and then they hand you a check. I consider this "next-level" privilege. Seriously, you do what you love, and you get paid. With privilege comes responsibility. You have to be good as a speaker, trainer, teacher, and coach. If there's one thing I've stressed as a speakers' coach and a speaker myself, it's that no one is all things to all people; you need to find something that you are excellent at and share that message.

Most of us are appalled at people who enter the speaking circuit with no new message. Rehashing other speakers' material is akin to doing a music rendition of a famous cover; it's not yours, maybe you made it better but, in the end, you don't leave your mark because you didn't create it. Somebody else owns the rights and will take the money all the way to the bank. Once they sue you and take your money and ruin your name.

In my years of speaking, I met a man who was moderately successful in business, *he had some well-known, spectacular failures as well.*

Through business connections he had befriended a national speaker; this speaker, unfortunately, was unwell and soon after the two met, he passed away. And somewhere in that connection my friend was given the library of speeches, stories, quotes, and sayings of this former national speaker.

I remember him calling me saying, "just like" me, he wants to be a speaker. After a few hours of heart-to-heart discussions, he (and his wife) decided this probably wasn't the job for him.

See he wanted to be on the stage, but he didn't know or, frankly, want to believe that before you ever hit the stage, you sit in airports and medium-grade hotels and spend many lonely nights of dinner in your room, all for an hour or two in the limelight. More importantly, he had nothing new to say. What he had was a few verbatim, rehashed ideas from other famous speakers littered with a few of his glory-day football stories and a few embellished hard luck stories that he liked to tell. He had been a "good old boy" local college football player and people knew him, and he was generally likable, but like so many middle-aged, late-in-life, wannabe speakers his questionable business practices through the years had made him friends … and enemies.

He thought he could make it on the national speaking circuit because he had another speaker's material, he thought he could claim it and make it work for him. He didn't know anything about the material he had been given, because he had never gone through the fire of crafting a speech, recrafting, and rewriting and researching to make a connection with this audience. What makes some speakers better than others is the privilege of hard work alone in your office working on your presentation over and over and over.

Very few speakers are successful when their adult life has been easy. What brings most of us to the stage are life lessons that we want to help our audience circumnavigate, because we've actually been there, and we don't want our audience to have to go there, so we share how to bypass the troubled water and sail smoothly to a safe harbor.

There's another side to privilege that speakers have that we would do well to acknowledge, and it falls in line with trust and honesty. Without these two aspects, your audience will know and they most likely will not return or tell others to follow you.

In today's world, unlike even a few years ago, you will be found, followed, watched, hounded even, and for some, if you're not careful, your truth will be posted online. Social media has absolutely, unequivocally changed our industry. I now teach other speakers how to survive in an online world that will crush you, because it can.

Now I'm not here to scare you. I'm just here to remind you to do your job, do it well, be amazing, and let others come to your defense when someone who hides behind a keyboard decides they just don't like you that day.

Remember with your privilege as a speaker comes responsibility and in today's cancel culture, they will hold you under a microscope to vet every aspect of your ability, your intelligence, your stories, your facts, and your figures make sure you are who you say you are.

In other words, you're never gonna pull off "wearing mom jeans," if you've never been a mom. People typically don't like it when you disagree with them, and typically, this goes double when it's in public. The old saying: "Praise in public; criticize in private" is especially true as a speaker.

7

STAYING POWER

Speaking comes easy to me. It always has. My guess is it always will. I'm most comfortable on a stage in front of audience; it's where even on my worst days, I'm at my best. I'm the sort of speaker who lifts her audiences up. I sway mindsets. I get people to think differently, and I get them to react with a goal that inspires them to take action. I'm really good at communicating, so good that I like to think that communication is my superpower. It's what I do and do well, and so it's strange that somehow, years ago, I somehow got it in my head that since I was an able speaker, I wasn't a writer — at least, not a capable writer.

Nothing could be further from the truth, or as my editor once told me, "When we write down exactly what we say, exactly how we say it, writing is easy." Broken down in those terms was an "aha!" moment, and so I offer to those who want to write a book — for anyone who wants an additional revenue stream and has something to say — go for it. Even if writing has been hard for you in the past, if you can speak, writing will come easy.

And, if you're a keynote speaker, then learning to write and writing well will serve you for the long haul. In fact, I can't really think of anyone who's killing it on the speaker circuits who hasn't added *author* to their credentials. Now, certainly, this isn't a hard and fast rule, but if I were to put my finger on the one element that proved to be a game changer for me, it's that my book, *Speak Without Fear*, opened a lot of doors. I was already teaching public speaking at Harvard University as a guest lecturer and was a long-time faculty trainer at The Campaign School at Yale University, but it certainly added to my cache and proved to be a valuable revenue stream.

Authoring a book gives keynotes credibility. I found that it cemented my position as an expert in the field of public speaking. Writing a book gives you credibility. It gives your ideas permanence in the mind of the beholder. Look at it this way: If you were hiring someone to speak at your event, would you hire the speaker who has written a book on her business or the one who hasn't? It's interesting, though, because a book under your belt also makes you more accessible as an expert. Not everyone can afford to come to a speaking event, and not everyone will take the time, even virtually. But everyone can get online and buy a book, then download it on their favorite app and read it or listen anywhere they want to, whenever they have the time. Books are inexpensive, and they give people a high return on investment.

In addition to all that, writing is the best way to say something and not be interrupted. It's long-form communication that people can take with them and refer back to again and again. With the mess the news media and a lot of popular podcasts have gotten themselves into taking things out of context and editing things down, people are eager for all the information, and time to process it. They want to know the whole story.

Even more compelling, I found in writing my first book that it forced me to refine and finesse my ideas. The process helped me better communicate — and as I've said before, I was already good at it. But there's always room for improvement. Writing a book got me to look at my material through fresh eyes and come up with different angles and examples to appeal to a wider range of readers and clients.

Finally, a book gives you a bigger audience. It gave me platforms in a number of new areas that either sell books or, in the case of social media, are friendly to different products and mediums — think book reviewers, book clubs, etc. Having a product to sell gets people to engage with your other content, and this increases the likelihood that they will remember you, recommend you, share your profile or content with other followers. It comes down to content and content marketing and finding new, compelling ways to promote your message and mission.

OUTLINING

When I decided in 2005 that a book would be a good investment as a "heavy" business card, and this was after years of people nudging and prodding me to write one, I was cautious. For years, the idea of writing a book came down to answering the age-old question of whether the world needed another book on public speaking. There are plenty of them out there. It wasn't enough that people said, "Nobody teaches like you do, Deb." For me it came down to experiencing an awful keynote speaker.

This guy was the worst. His message was teaspoon deep. He had no stage presence. I leaned over to a friend and asked, "The audience isn't listening. The cameraman can't follow this guy for his stupid speaker tricks of walking around the room and not focusing on the audience. How did he get to be the keynote speaker?" I'll never forget her response: "Well, Deb, he has a book." I thought to myself if that's what it takes for an awful speaker to get the keynote job then that was enough for me to stop being lazy, do the hard work, focus, find an editor, and start writing my book; no excuses — no matter what it takes.

As much as I wanted the additional revenue stream and for the people who came to hear me speak be able to take something with them to reiterate what I'd taught them, I didn't know where to begin. Possibly the biggest hurdle for me was to carve out the time, but once I committed to the process, making the book a priority got easier. And, if I'm being honest, besides the years I spent putting it off, once I made it a priority, the writing came easier too.

Writing a book is a lot like crafting a speech. Sure, it's longer, but there are a lot of similarities. For starters, the very first step I take in writing a speech is to think about nailing down, conceptually at least, a beginning, a middle, and an end. All great speeches have these three components, and typically, books follow a similar model. Now, for our purposes, I'll limit what insight I have on bookmaking to nonfiction.

For most speakers, and I don't want to pigeon-hole anyone, the books they'll pen are in the genres of self-help, memoir, or how-to.

This is where some preliminary research can be helpful. It's a good idea to read some books in your genre or subject area, because most of them follow a formula that has been proven to be successful. Chances are you already have books in your library that fit this bill, that you perhaps refer to regularly. Reread them, this time with an eye for structure and outline. Some of you, I know, may find that with practice, you can freestyle your speaking engagements. Well, you can't freestyle a book, at least not entirely! A good nonfiction book needs a good outline so you don't repeat yourself and so you can space out your content. It also helps you make sure you have enough content for a full book.

As for analogies, imagine dumping on a table as many jigsaws as you have chapters. You want each chapter to perfectly capture your topic as its own image; you also want each chapter to complement the overall picture. Use commonsense and consider your potential readers. What will your reader need to know as a building block? Is this a step-by-step how-to guide? If so, start from the beginning and chronologically plot milestones. If this is a topic-driven book, then consider a natural progression to introduce key themes to readers. Make notes of subheadings and introductory topics as they come to mind.

Of course, you can have periods of writing freestyle — that's how you develop your writing voice. This is where you write what you want to say without trying to impress anyone or get all the grammar correct or even make sense. You want to get the thoughts out of your head first; you can clean them up later. My editor gave me the best writing advice I ever got. She directed me to "Write what you say."

This is where you may begin to see that writing a book can be fun. It's not *all* fun, and it certainly isn't easy, but I was surprised to find that, just like speaking, I could enjoy myself when I really got into the groove of writing what I really wanted to say, in my own voice. Of course, this didn't happen overnight, and it didn't happen without some help. Just as I am an expert in my field of public speaking, someone else is an expert in how to write a book. It's never a bad idea to get a writing coach or developmental editor to help you outline, hone, and tweak at whatever level you need. And I'll go ahead and say this right now: there's nothing wrong with dictating your content. If you're already a speaker, then try speaking your book! You can have it transcribed by a number of apps and then go through it yourself or get the help of an editor.

PREWRITING

Once I was able to articulate a beginning, middle, and end to my potential book, I began to review the years of content I had. Ends up I had a lot. I had so much content that I couldn't see the forest for the trees. This was daunting. I couldn't even figure out what I should include in the book and what I should leave out. I also couldn't put my finger on what my book's "hook" should be.

Prewriting is a big part of discovering your hook. Before you begin to write, take a week to think and make notes about your subject, your potential genres, and what distinguishes you and your message from everyone else. This is not necessarily stuff that's going to make the cut in your final draft, but your book certainly won't get written without it. F. Scott Fitzgerald said, "You don't write because you want to say something, you write because you have something to say." So, what is it? What is it you want to tell your readers? What is it you want to say? What part or parts of your message are the most relevant today? Are there already books out there in the market that might be similar? How is yours different? Why are you the person to author this book?

This is your elevator speech or as I tell my audience your BEE (Big Fat Claim, Explain, Example), your mission statement. It's going to help bring you back to the point when you lose your focus or get writer's block.

You may find that during the prewriting stage it's helpful to have someone to act as a sounding board. It can be another professional in your field or just a good friend you like to bounce ideas off of. Of course, as I've said, it can also be a professional writer or editor. And you might consider that someone who isn't familiar with your material could be the best sounding board. You've heard the saying "Write what you know." Well, I think it goes a little bit further than that. I think the trick is to write what you know while you assume or pretend your readers don't know anything. This doesn't mean to treat them like they're unintelligent. It does mean that you should break things down into their simplest pieces, like deconstructing them, and then show how they build on each other to create *the* idea or concept that is at the heart of your book. Someone who doesn't already work in your field or know your material backward and forward is an ideal person to talk things through with because they will immediately pick out things that are confusing or unclear.

One thing I've learned as well is that whether or not they are reading fiction or nonfiction, people love stories. Do you start some of your speeches with a particular story? Some of my favorite TED Talks begin this way, a story that gets the listener engaged and illustrates the entire point of the speech. Humor and suspense are your friends here or both, however you can swing it. Whether your audience is listening or reading, storytelling, humor, and suspense are what's going to keep them entertained.

I can remember when I first sat down to write my book. It seemed overwhelming. I knew if I could put into the book some of what I teach from the stage, it would be a good first start.

As I was writing, one thing I noticed from the very beginning, and so did my editor, is I tend to repeat myself. I realized the reason I do is from my years on the stage; you must repeat your thought so your audience will grasp what you're saying. Unfortunately, you can't do that in a book, so you must figure out what your big theme is going to be and what it is you want your legacy to be. A book is what you leave behind when you walk off the stage.

I was fortunate to find the right team at the very beginning to help me plan out my first book and now this one. Although I struggled in the beginning with the concept of writing a book, because as I've mentioned before I felt there were plenty of books on public speaking, but one thing my editor kept saying that really made me stop and think is that no one teaches the way I do, and I know my way works. I have hundreds, if not thousands, of clients who prove my method can make anyone a better speaker.

So, *Speak Without Fear* was written. Now, what's interesting is that book is a few years old, and what I've learned in that time is that I can teach you all the rules to being a great speaker, but when things go wrong or when you're put in new positions that you've never been in before because you're not used to being on stage, somebody needs to tell you the rules. That's what prompted this new book.

I found that too many good people didn't understand the rules of being a great speaker because no one ever told or taught them. Frankly it's something that some speakers I think like to hold close to their chest because they're so afraid of competition, but as you've read 100 times in this book that I want you to be your very best. I'm not worried about you because I'm not worried about me. What I'd like for you to be able to see in the pages of this book is to have the permission to command the stage in every way, so your audience leaves better then when you found them.

Writing, or in this case, "speaking" your book aloud comes down to asking the right questions in the right order. If you do your job in Week #1 (Pre-writing) and Week #2 (Q & A), Week #3 (Writing and Revising) and Week #4 (Self-editing) will be exponentially easier for you, so don't rush things. In the end, it's a matter of forming the right questions within each chapter.

Week #1: Pre-writing

Day 1: Craft a Mission Statement
Be able to sum up your book and its purpose in a single sentence. As an example, let's say you want to write a book to advocate the value of prescribed burns. Your mission statement might be something like: This book helps readers better understand the value of prescribed burns to protect our communities, reduce the risk of wildfires, rebalance reforestation, and protect drinking watersheds.

Day 2: Create an Outline
Take a macro approach to organize your content. List key concepts and talking points.

Day 3: Create a Table of Contents

Following your outline cues, choose your chapters and title them. In keeping with the above illustration, perhaps your table of contents include chapters like: Chapter 1: Our forests are wildly out of balance, Chapter 2: Wildfires are becoming more intense, Chapter 3: Science is on our side, Chapter 4: Fire promotes the growth of trees, wildflowers, and other plants.

Day 4: Finalize Table of Contents

Using your table of content as your guide, add subheadings. A good rule of thumb is to have three to four subsections per chapter; if you don't have but two or three subsections, consider whether or not you have enough content to fill an entire chapter. This is key. Few things are worse than when a writer sits down to write and lacks enough content to create a cohesive and compelling chapter. With the theme, Chapter 3: Science is on our side. The best way to reduce the risk of catastrophic wildfire is to restore our forests to their natural state with controlled or prescribed burns. Chapter 4: After many years of fire exclusion, an ecosystem that needs periodic fire becomes unhealthy. Trees are stressed by overcrowding; fire-dependent species disappear; and flammable fuels build up and become hazardous.

Day 5: Pose 100 Questions

Following your finalized table of content, begin thinking about how you should go about interviewing yourself and what questions you should ask. These "questions" can also be written as writing prompts and nudges. For example, your first chapter might be about who you are and who should read your book. This chapter's questions might include: Q1: You live in a city, why should you care about forest management? Q2: A brief history of my years as a water commissioner and what I learned. Q3: How we all should view prescribed burns in the in age of nimby, or "not in my backyard." Q4: Understanding fire, the fear, the flame, and the rebirth. Q5: If you have ever wondered about the role of prescribed burns in your watershed or for land management, this book is your resource. Q6: This book is based in science and proven wildfire mitigation and preparedness strategies.

Day 6: Pose Another 100 Questions

Do not repeat anecdotes. Let's again say your book is about the value of prescribed burns. Another chapter's questions might be: Q41: How fire reduces hazardous fuels? Q42: Did you know that fire minimizes the spread of pest insects and disease? Q43: Fire removes unwanted species that threaten species native to an ecosystem? Q44: Fire provides food for wildlife. Q45: In SC fire improves habitat for the Oconee Bell, rare flower of the southern Appalachians found in our watershed. Q46: Elaborate on why fire promotes the growth of trees, wildflowers, plants, and insects. Q47: What are the stages of producing a prescribed burn plan for your watershed? Q48: How and why are these stages important? Q49: What else should readers know about these stages?

Day 7: Finalize a Series of 300 Questions

Dig deep for new content. As a general rule of thumb, 300 well-considered questions yield between 35,000 to 50,000-word manuscript.

Week #2: Q & A

Day 1: Fifty Questions

Download a transcription app that allows you to record your voice and transcribe what you've said. Self-interviewing — at least in the beginning — is super weird, but after an hour or so, you'll get the hang of it.

Day 2: Fifty Questions

Inevitably, once you start getting more comfortable interviewing yourself, which can be awkward at first, you'll think of other things to add. It's a good idea to have an "add" word. This allows you to be able to use "find and replace" feature to track down material that you know at the outset during an interview you'll be moving to a different section. To ensure its practicality, use a word that stands out from the rest of the document's general theme.

Day 3: Fifty Questions

Tip: Speak clearly. You'll likely pay per minute, but mumbling makes for a sketchy foundation. Articulate well your words and phrases.

Day 4: Fifty Questions

Tip: Again, you can always cut and paste; the key is to have it recorded and have it transcribed.

Day 5: Fifty Questions

Tip: When in doubt, ask yourself: Why and/or how? Why does something matter? How is it relevant?

Day 6: Fifty Questions

Tip: It's always, always, always better to have content you might end up cutting than it is to be missing content altogether.

Day 7: Transcription

Most transcription services have a relatively quick turnaround, some as quick as twenty-four hours. Once you receive your transcript, it's time to begin writing and revising it. If you're a true do-it-yourselfer and decide to transcribe your files yourself, begin self-editing as you type.

Week #3: Writing and Revising Tips

Day 1: Create a "Blank" Document

Cut and paste your six transcripts into a single blank document. In follow general formatting guidelines, skip any and all frills. Don't change indentation, use double-spaced Times New Roman, size-12 font. Do not use hard returns to create breaks between chapters or subheadings. Do not cut and paste anything from the Internet.

Day 2: Spelling and Grammar Check
Perform a perfunctory grammar and spellcheck using whichever word processing application you're using to write your book. At this early stage, it can be a pretty tedious endeavor, but it's a terrific way to peruse the entire manuscript to pinpoint "mechanic" issues and identify transcription irregularities, etc.

Day 3: Review How Chapters Begin and End
Think of each chapter as a separate vignette. Very similar to the arc of a book itself, each chapter should have its own distinct sense of theme and offer readers a beginning, middle, and end. Ensure that the end of one chapter leads effortlessly to the next.

Day 4: Add Transitional Phrases
Start at the beginning and review your manuscript. Add transitional phrases and sentences between paragraphs and ideas.

Day 5: Cut and Rearrange
When you come across a tangential passage, cut, and paste it into a separate document. Some of what your "slush" document has might be used elsewhere — or, I've found, proves to be an opportunity for a second and third book.

Day 6: Imagery
Use language that paints a picture for your readers. Editors often say rather than telling you readers, show them. The goal is to use as few adverbs as you can.

Day 7: Style
There are different style guides; it doesn't matter so much one your book follows as long as there's uniformity and consistency,

e.g., if you use % in one place don't write percentage out in another.

Week #4: Self-editing Tips

Day 1: Avoid Using Passive Voice

Passive voice describes sentences that convey who or what is receiving the action, rather than performing the action within the sentence. Active sentences display who or what is performing the action and are commonly preferred. While passive voice can be used sparingly, over usage results in flat or less interesting text for your reader. You can spot passive voice by looking for sentences with verb phrases that include is, was, are, were, or been. Passive: The girl was scratched by the cat. Active: The cat scratched the girl.

Day 2: Ensure Nouns and Pronouns Agree

Do not use *they* in reference to a singular noun. Incorrect: *A person can choose any book they like.* Correct: *A person can choose any book she likes.* Correct: *People can choose any books they like.*

Day 3: Accuracy

Keep in mind that spellcheck helps with accuracy but isn't failproof. Watch out for any and all typos. Words may have been inadvertently spelled phonetically either in writing or during transcription. As in, I like two right. I like to right. I like to write.

Day 4: Gender-neutral Language

Use *humankind* instead of *mankind*. Use language that's inclusive to the reader: *we or you* are appropriate if used consistently and accurately.

Day 5: Parenthetical Elements

Commas set off parenthetical elements if a slight break is intended. If a stronger break is needed or if there are commas within the parenthetical element, em dashes or parentheses should be used. An adverb essential to the meaning of the clause (as in the last two examples below) should not be enclosed in commas, e.g. This, indeed, was exactly what he had feared would happen. This road leads away from, rather than toward, your destination. The storehouse was indeed empty. Two students cheated and were therefore disqualified.

Day 6: Subjunctive vs. Indicative

Note that not every *if* takes a subjunctive verb: when the action or state might be true, but the writer does not know, the indicative is called for, e.g., If I was right about this, please call. If Napoleon was in fact poisoned with arsenic, historians will need to reconsider his associates.

Day 7: Restrictive and nonrestrictive phrases

A phrase that is restrictive, that is, essential to the meaning of the noun it belongs to, should not be set off by commas. A nonrestrictive phrase, however, should be enclosed in commas or, if at the end of a sentence, preceded by a comma, e.g. The woman wearing a red coat is my sister. My sister, wearing a red coat, set off for the city. She set off for the city, wearing a red coat. Another example: The Bible says that anyone who claims to be in the light but is hostile toward his co-worker is still in the darkness. Read the sentence without "but is hostile toward his co-worker." It does not mean the same thing; therefore, commas are not used.

PRE-PRESS

These days, authors can work with some exciting publishing professionals. Keep in mind the cost to do this varies, and when you hire a publishing consultant or book doctor, my experience is, like most things in life, one gets what she pays for. I cannot stress how valuable it was to work with a content/developmental editor. I also cannot stress how important it is to understand the elements of your book. Include title page, table of contents, list of contributors, list of illustrations, glossary, foreword or preface, notes, and bibliography.

When I speak to the production process, we're focused on what happens after you have a first draft. After self-editing, as a rough guide for a non-complex, project-managed book, the prepress stages include copy-editing, typesetting, proofreading, revisions, final corrections, and final file creation, including, among others, a press-ready file and an ePub file, there's the actual printing and delivery of bound copies.

As for copyediting, copyeditors correct grammar, spelling, and syntax; check references for inconsistencies; bring any suspected errors, omissions, or duplications to the publisher's attention. Copyeditors do not intervene when it comes to stylistic measures other than to implement an agreed style; copyeditors do not undertake any rewriting or restructuring or check for factual errors. Permissions, you must obtain permission for any third-party materials cited that fall outside the of "fair use." This goes for artwork and images.

You can expect to pay a few thousand dollars for your manuscript to be fully developmentally edited. Some proofreaders charge per page, but for a 50,000-word manuscript, you can expect to pay a cent or two per word to proofread. You can expect to pay anywhere from a hundred to a few thousand for a book cover. For those who say we can't judge a book by its cover, I, for one, admit to making book purchases on the sole datum that I found the cover compelling or clever or really pretty.

There are many predatory publishing services, so vetting is critical. Have a good rapport with your publishing team. If you work with a hybrid or vanity press, your manuscript will be cleaned and polished, but your work might not be developed to its true potential. In other words, while hybrid publishers go through mechanics of editing, it's up to you, the author, to make your book different, to make it stand out, and to make certain your voice isn't muddled or lost through the process.

Here's the math. For a 50,000-word manuscript, you can expect to pay anywhere between a dollar to a dollar and half per minute for online transcription services. Rev.com offers an exemplary streamlined experience, wherein the transcribers remove the false starts of ums and ahs, which ultimately saves author's time. Regarding budgeting and financial forecasting, and this is a guesstimate, let's assume that to answer fifty questions takes two hours, so for six days of answering for a total of three hundred questions, at a dollar and a quarter, transcription services will run around $900. (This is a 2022 estimate)

Think like a big five publisher. It takes a full year. They print Advanced Readers Copies ARCs. This is paramount. Don't get yourself canceled. The sales cycle for your book begins before it's completed. Promotional copy and cover design need to be agreed ahead of publication. Don't rush to market. You never get a second chance to make a first impression.

I can't stress enough the value of having authored a book. It took a good deal of effort and time and money; even more compelling is the fact that if 10 percent of authoring a book is writing, the other 90 percent of authoring a book is marketing it, but more than any other indicator, I chalk my success, my staying power, to the four books I've written and published over the last decade.

THERE'S NO LUCK IN BEING LEGENDARY

It took time for me to change the perception of myself from a speaker to a writer. Oftentimes people refer to me as a *motivational speaker*, but that's not what I think I am. I like to think of myself as a *motivational teacher*. As a teacher and speech coach, that's my job. I take it seriously, and I do it well. There is nothing I dislike more than when a speaker works to rally an audience to make them feel good during their presentation but leaves the stage without the audience remembering anything they heard or having some sort of actionable items to change their life. Sure, they were entertained for an hour if they're lucky, but ultimately, it's a waste of everyone's time.

Speakers who fail to generate meaningful content will fail to secure lasting success. To me, that means my audience has to have actionable items they can glean from my meeting or conference and put into practice that day. Are you motivated? Absolutely. Have you learned something? Yes. Do you feel good? I hope so. I really do, but that wasn't the purpose of our time together. Listen, ice cream makes me feel good, hanging with friends and going to concerts makes me feel good; the difference is when I can teach someone to communicate more effectively.

In the current self-improvement world, we have a few new players. One has a rule about the first few seconds of your day, another former sports star who was injured and has a podcast and still another created an energy bar and did super well has now set himself (and his wife) up as dispensers of knowledge with their own TV show and he interviews his friends who are doing the same thing. No doubt it would be great to be on stage with your new famous friends, but in the real speaking work (not made for TV because you can afford to create and produce your own show) life doesn't work like that. And the flame-out will be spectacular albeit sad because of few in the circle seem like people of good will. My point is this: when the lights come up and the show is over what will your audience take home with them to use that day or the next? If you have no answer, rework your material and craft deeper knowledge to change lives.

Maybe you were made for TV. I hope so, I really do but, in the meantime, the best way to get to the bright lights and big time is to create a lasting message or to retool your message for today's audience. Pivot is the name of the game to keep relevant in the marketplace.

In the speaking business, there's a phrase many of us use called "staying power," and what we mean by it is your relevancy on the circuit is only as strong as your message is relevant to the people you're speaking to.

Throughout the book I've given examples of people who started out strong, but now we don't hear from them anymore. Maybe they got tired, maybe they got sick, maybe they found another opportunity, or maybe they just chose to step back from being a road warrior. Goodness knows the older you get, the more you like to sleep in your own bed and not another lumpy hotel bed with cheap sheets, plastic cups, and little soaps.

To have staying power in this field boils down to the overriding theme that you have a message that resonates with your audience every time you stand and speak. It may sound unusual, but I don't want to be the type of writer, speaker, or coach who make it seem like speaking on the circuit nationally or internationally is all fun and games. Don't get me wrong. It is, but the truth is you spend more time in airports and hotels than you ever do on a stage and consider this: You're only paid for the time you're on stage and perform.

Staying power comes down to the strength of your message to any audience that hears it. Repeatedly, I have mentioned that you must keep up with the times, you must keep perfecting your message, and nowadays, you've got to be good on social media. Gone are the days where just a good name would get you to the stage. Because so many people are clamoring for the stage, you've got to have something in your message and your stories and your messages of encouragement that stands out.

Without a doubt, public speaking is a brutal business. Whether someone undercut you on price, whether somebody just doesn't know you, whether the conference director chooses to go in a different direction, or whether your topic just isn't the topic de jure of the day, there's a lot to strategize.

Storytelling is one of those topics that goes in and out of vogue every eight to ten years. Back and forth the pendulum swings then we get too technical. We forget the personal side that people want to connect to, so we swing it back to the technical, because we got too mushy and didn't have a message when we got personal, and then it swings back again.

You've got to keep up with the times, you must. In a sense, look down the road and figure out the issues you and your audience will be potentially come up against. I can remember when Covid-19 hit. Pretty much everything shut down. Nobody was speaking. There were no stage events. There was really nothing for a speaker to do except write and rewrite their material and clean it up, be active on social media, and try to keep up with their clients and friends. In one year, our industry changed, and it changed in a massive way.

Folks say they're fatigued with Zoom, and yet conference organizers realize it's a whole lot cheaper to keep you at home looking at the camera than flying you to Cancun to speak for an hour. Corporate offices have changed because more people are working from home.

I don't know what the future holds, but I do know that you're going to have to learn some new skills to keep up. You're going to have to do things you probably never thought you would, to keep your income where it should be. You're going to have to give a little bit more, because this industry is full of people who're willing to do just enough to get by. Because of this unexpected overhaul in the marketplace, the financial model for speakers will most likely change. I encourage you to do the extras. Things like writing a book, building your blog, hosting a radio show, or creating a new line that allows you to stand out from the others.

I can remember when I first started in the business. All conferences were held on the weekend. You flew in on a Friday; you spoke on Saturday; you flew home Sunday. After a while no conferences were held on the weekends because the public didn't want to give up their weekends. So now you fly in on a Sunday you speak Monday or Tuesday, and you are home Wednesday. Every few years, it's a very different world, and you've got to keep up with what the industry demands. More than anything, when it comes to securing a lasting speaking career, it isn't the strongest who survive, it's those of us who are nimble.

I have a talk I give on the circuit. Its theme is one's ability to have staying power, and it centers on the incomparable Lucille Ball, who at fifteen, made her way to Manhattan to enroll in John Murray Anderson's Acting School. After one term, she received a letter from the school saying she didn't have what it takes to be an actress, and it would be a waste of her money to continue. From Day 1, she was told she had no talent and, after auditioning, failed to get into four Broadway chorus lines. To make a living, she became a model for commercial photographers. In 1933, she won national attention as the Chesterfield Cigarette girl.

This break got her to Hollywood as a Goldwyn chorus girl. For the next two years she played unbilled, bit roles in twenty-four movies. She then spent seven years at RKO, where she got leading roles in low-budget movies. In all, she appeared in seventy-two B-movies before she, at the age of thirty-seven, became too old to be "credible" as a female love-interest. Her lackluster career on the silver screen ended without fanfare in 1948, and she swallowed her pride and became Liz Cooper on the live radio show, "My Favorite Husband." Her then director, Jess Oppenheimer, gave her a couple of tickets to the "Jack Benny Show" and said, "I want you to go back to school." When she returned to the studio for the next rehearsal, she gushed with enthusiasm, and at that next session, she hammed it up. The audience roared their approval, and Lucy Ricardo was born.

In 1951, a middle-aged Lucy leaped out from our black-and-white television screens into every living room in America. Susan Lacy, executive producer of "American Masters" said, "To say that Lucille Ball was a phenomenon is an understatement. Through sheer determination and hard work, this one woman fundamentally changed the broadcast industry forever."

Most people, when they finally become successful, become unadventurous. Fearful of losing what they've gained, they abandon the behaviors that brought them success but not Lucy. As the fearless owner of her own TV studio, she took enormous chances both professionally and financially on two new concept TV shows: one was out of this world, a little show called "Star Trek" and the other, true to her life story, was "Mission: Impossible." American television would never be the same.

On April 27, 1989, the *New York Times* ran her obituary. Its last few sentences were these: "Addressing a group of would-be actors, Lucille Ball said the best way to get along with tough directors was "Don't die when they knock you down." In other words, have the power to stay.

I credit my staying power to the fact that teaching never goes out of style. And in the corporate world, everyone is always going to be speaking. Most people will deal with the media, and in their lifetime, there will be a crisis at their company. So, I have crafted into the work that I do a lifetime of work opportunities because I stayed with the basics. Yes, I have several speeches on leadership, and getting out of your own way, and finding the light in the darkness. I have a very positive outlook as a speaker, I'm an encouraging speaker, I'm a kick in the seat of the pants speaker, but my bread and butter fall under the tenets of public speaking and public speaking training in all aspects. It's what I love, and it's what I'm good at.

As Lucille Ball stated so powerfully, "Love yourself first and everything else falls into line. You really have to love yourself to get anything done in this world." Staying power takes believing in yourself, knowing what you teach, what you do, and how you do it. Believing in yourself is so beneficial to your audience that you can do nothing else.

I am guessing you picked up this book because you know you have the gift of speaking, and without a doubt, you have a lot to offer an audience who needs to hear your message. I wanted to leave a legacy in a book form for others to find their way to the stage and stand in the light, to hear the audience laugh and cheer, and to stand as they acknowledge your gift that you shared with them as you leave the stage.

Do the work, make the time, be your best self, not because others expect you to be but because you know you can be and now you know the rules for the road that leads to a lifetime of success.

As a speaker I don't think there's anything more important in life then giving a bit of yourself to help somebody do well in life. It is perhaps the greatest gift you will leave behind. For some speaking might be your job, but I hope that over time you begin to speak more so you can help other people find their path because you lit the way for others to follow. This is what perfecting your platform is all about, your ability to transform your stage presence into stage power for a lifetime.

ABOUT THE AUTHOR

Deb Sofield is a dynamic and engaging keynote speaker and executive speech coach with over thirty years of experience in training women and men for success in public speaking, presentation skills, crisis communications, media skills and message development in the U.S. and abroad. She is the author of the book, *Speak without Fear – Rock Star Presentation Skills to get People to Hear What You Say*, and *Encouragement For Your Life ~ Tough Love Memos to Help You Fight Your Battles and Change the World* vol. 1-3. Deb hosts her own radio talk show on the Salem Network.

Deb is the CEO of Executive Speech Coaching, a private speech coaching company with decades of experience helping clients become effective, powerful communicators with a polished message for success in every medium. As a former advertising agency owner, Sofield blends visual and verbal messaging that wins at every level.

She prepares and guides elected officials, candidates, and senior leadership by working one-on-one to build their skills and refine their personal speaking style and public persona for success in speeches, debates, media interviews, webcasts, radio, public panels, and TED Talks. She tailors training to the event and to the audience by on-camera practice, mock interviews, and debate rehearsals.

Deb believes that to be successful in today's twitter-infused marketplace, you must know how to craft your message, be able to articulate your vision, understand your audience and learn how to master the microphone, lectern, and stage.

She has been a visiting professor, teaching public speaking at Harvard University's Kennedy School of Government – Women in Public Policy Program, and as faculty for The Campaign School at Yale University, where she is past president of the board. For years she has worked with the International Republican Institute and served on the board for the Women's Democracy Network. She taught Communications and Media Training for Civil Society around the world and has served as a mentor and trainer for the Center for Liberty in the Middle East.

Deb Sofield is one of only a few trainers in the marketplace who also has experience as an elected official. She is a Commissioner of Public Works for the Greenville Water System and is the first woman to hold this position since its inception in 1918. She was formerly a two-term member of Greenville City Council.

Beyond just business and politics, Deb is a recognized for her work for improving the lives of others and her contribution to the state of South Carolina, the southern region, and the nation, Sofield was honored by Leadership South Carolina with *Legacy of Leadership Award*. Considered one of South Carolinas most formidable women, the Southeastern Institute for Women in Politics awarded Deb Sofield the *Leading Women Award*. Sofield was also awarded the *Order of the Palmetto* – by the Governor, the State of South Carolina's highest honor. She was named *"Communicator of the Year"* by the Association for Women in Communications and won the *Toastmasters District 58 Communication and Leadership Award* for the state of South Carolina. She was also awarded the *Thurmond Excellence in Public Service honor* and as a YWCA Woman of Achievement. Sofield was chosen as the *ATHENA Award* recipient by the Greenville Chamber of Commerce for her work at home and abroad.

Deb Sofield is a Liberty Fellow – affiliated with the Aspen Institute Global Leadership Network, a worldwide community of successful, high-integrity entrepreneurial leaders. Deb holds a BA in public speaking.

For more information visit: http://www.debsofield.com

Soft Landings

- I agree with you
- You make an interesting point
- I appreciate your position
- I understand your point of view
- I can see where you are coming from
- Many people I have spoken to feel as you do
- Yes, we need to look into that more carefully
- Your point is well taken
- I can see why you would think that way

Transitions

- First, let me say
- I don't have that information, **but** I can tell you
- You should also know that
- Let me explain
- I'm also frequently asked
- Let me add
- A common concern is
- For example
- Equally importantly
- One point I believe the audience would be interested in
- You can go one step further...

NOTE: Do not follow a soft landing with the word **"But" or "However"** those words start a fight

Made in the USA
Middletown, DE
14 April 2022